Behavior and Dam Passage of Juvenile Chinook Salmon at Cougar Reservoir and Dam, Oregon, March 2011–February 2012

By John W. Beeman, Hal C. Hansel, Amy C. Hansen, Philip V. Haner, Jamie M. Sprando, Collin D. Smith, Scott D. Evans, and Tyson W. Hatton

Prepared in cooperation with the U.S. Army Corps of Engineers

Open-File Report 2013–1079

U.S. Department of the Interior
U.S. Geological Survey

U.S. Department of the Interior
KEN SALAZAR, Secretary

U.S. Geological Survey
Suzette M. Kimball, Acting Director

U.S. Geological Survey, Reston, Virginia: 2013

For more information on the USGS—the Federal source for science about the Earth,
its natural and living resources, natural hazards, and the environment—visit
http://www.usgs.gov or call 1–888–ASK–USGS

For an overview of USGS information products, including maps, imagery, and publications,
visit *http://www.usgs.gov/pubprod*

To order this and other USGS information products, visit *http://store.usgs.gov*

Suggested citation:
Beeman, J.W., Hansel, H.C., Hansen, A.C., Haner, P.V., Sprando, J.M., Smith, C.D., Evans, S.D., and Hatton, T.W.,
2013, Behavior and dam passage of juvenile Chinook salmon at Cougar Reservoir and Dam, Oregon, March 2011–
February 2012: U.S. Geological Survey Open-File Report 2013-1079, 48 p.

Any use of trade, product, or firm names is for descriptive purposes only and does not imply
endorsement by the U.S. Government.

Contents

Figures

Tables

Conversion Factors and Datums

Conversion Factors

Inch/Pound to SI

Multiply	By	To obtain
foot (ft)	0.3048	meter (m)
foot per second (ft/s)	0.3048	meter per second (m/s)
foot per minute (ft/min)	0.3048	meter per minute (m/min)
cubic foot per second (ft^3/s)	0.02832	cubic meter per second (m^3/s)

SI to Inch/Pound

Multiply	By	To obtain
millimeter (mm)	0.03937	inch (in.)
centimeter (cm)	0.3937	inch (in.)
meter (m)	3.281	foot (ft)
cubic meter (m^3)	35.31	cubic foot (ft^3)
kilometer (km)	0.6214	mile (mi)
kilometer (km)	0.5400	mile, nautical (nmi)
meter per second (m/s)	3.281	foot per second (ft/s)
milliliter (mL)	0.0002642	gallon (gal)
liter (L)	0.2642	gallon (gal)
gram (g)	0.03527	ounce, avoirdupois (oz)

Temperature in degrees Celsius ($°C$) may be converted to degrees Fahrenheit ($°F$) as follows:
$°F = (1.8 \times °C) + 32$

Datums

Vertical coordinate information is referenced to the National Geodetic Vertical Datum of 1929 (NGVD 29).
Horizontal coordinate information is referenced to the World Geodetic System of 1984 (WGS 84).
Elevation, as used in this report, refers to distance above vertical datum.
Concentrations of chemical constituents in water are given in milligrams per liter (mg/L).

Behavior and Dam Passage of Juvenile Chinook Salmon at Cougar Reservoir and Dam, Oregon, March 2011–February 2012

By John W. Beeman, Hal C. Hansel, Amy C. Hansen, Philip V. Haner, Jamie M. Sprando, Collin D. Smith, Scott D. Evans, and Tyson W. Hatton

Abstract

The movements and dam passage of juvenile Chinook salmon implanted with acoustic transmitters and passive integrated transponder tags were studied at Cougar Reservoir and Dam, near Springfield, Oregon. The purpose of the study was to provide information to aid with decisions about potential alternatives for improving downstream passage conditions for juvenile salmonids in this flood-control reservoir. In 2011, a total of 411 hatchery fish and 26 wild fish were tagged and released during a 3-month period in the spring, and another 356 hatchery fish and 117 wild fish were released during a 3-month period in the fall. A series of 16 autonomous hydrophones throughout the reservoir and 12 hydrophones in a collective system near the dam outlet were used to determine general movements and dam passage of the fish over the life of the acoustic transmitter, which was expected to be about 3 months. Movements within the reservoir were directional, and it was common for fish to migrate repeatedly from the head of the reservoir downstream to the dam outlet and back to the head of the reservoir. Most fish were detected near the temperature control tower at least once. The median time from release near the head of the reservoir to detection within about 100 meters of the dam outlet at the temperature control tower was between 5.7 and 10.8 days, depending on season and fish origin. Dam passage events occurred over a wider range of dates in the spring and summer than in the fall and winter, but dam passage numbers were greatest during the fall and winter. A total of 10.5 percent (43 of 411) of the hatchery fish and 15.4 percent (4 of 26) of the wild fish released in the spring are assumed to have passed the dam, whereas a total of 25.3 percent (90 of 356) of the hatchery fish and 16.9 percent (30 of 117) of the wild fish released in the fall are assumed to have passed the dam. A small number of fish passed the dam after their transmitters had stopped working and were detected at passive integrated transponder detectors at various locations downstream of the dam, indicating some tagged fish passed the dam undetected. The rate of dam passage was affected by diel period, discharge, and reservoir elevation. Diel period was the most influential factor of those examined, with nighttime dam passage rates about 9 times greater than daytime rates, depending on the distance of fish from the dam outlet. Dam passage rates also were positively related to dam discharge, and negatively related to reservoir elevation. In the operational condition used as an example, fish approached the dam outlet at the temperature control tower from the south and east and, when most fish got near the tower, they were directly in front of it. In many cases, the results for wild and hatchery fish were similar, or the results suggested hatchery fish could be reasonable surrogates for wild fish. Hatchery-origin and wild-origin fish behaved similarly in the following ways: their general movements in the reservoir; the timing of their dam passage; and the effects of diel period, discharge, and elevation on their passage rates.

Parasitic copepods were present on most wild fish examined, and the mortality of wild fish during capture, handling and tagging was much greater than that of hatchery fish. This suggests that the ability of wild fish to cope with stressors may be less than that of fish directly from the hatchery.

Introduction

The U.S. Army Corps of Engineers (COE) operates the Willamette Project (Project) in western Oregon, including a series of dams, revetments, and hatcheries. The primary purpose of the Project is flood control, but it also is operated to provide hydroelectricity, irrigation water, navigation, instream flows for wildlife, and recreation. The Project includes 13 dams, about 68 km of revetments, and several fish hatcheries. Cougar Dam and several other dams are located on tributaries of the Willamette River. The National Oceanic and Atmospheric Administration determined that the Project was jeopardizing the sustainability of anadromous fish stocks in the Willamette River Basin (National Oceanic and Atmospheric Administration, 2008)

Cougar Dam is a 158 m-high rock-fill dam on the South Fork of the McKenzie River about 63 km east of Springfield, Oregon. The dam, completed in 1964, is owned and operated by the COE. It has a hydraulic capacity of 1,050 ft^3/s and two Francis turbine units capable of generating a total of 25 megawatts. The reservoir is used primarily for flood control; therefore, the forebay elevation is maintained at high levels during summer months and low levels during winter months. A maximum conservation pool elevation of 1,690 ft National Geodetic Vertical Datum of 1929 (NGVD 29) typically is reached in May, and a minimum flood-control pool elevation of 1,532 ft is usually reached in December.

Water passes the dam over a spillway with Tainter gates or through a temperature control tower installed in 2005 (fig. 1). The spillway is not used as part of typical operations, so all water passing downstream normally goes through the temperature control tower. Prior to installation of the temperature control tower, water passing through the dam was drawn from deep within the reservoir and often was too cold for attraction and spawning of salmon downstream. The temperature control tower allows waters from various depths to be selectively passed through the dam to control downstream water temperatures. Water entering the temperature control tower can be passed through a flow regulating outlet (RO) and a powerhouse penstock. The RO intake is at elevation 1,478 ft, and the penstock to the turbines is at elevation 1,420 ft. A fish ladder and trapping facility completed in 2011 collects adult salmon in the tailrace for transportation upstream and provides the only means of upstream passage of adult salmon. As of 2013 there was no passage route designed for downstream passage of juvenile salmon; however, operational and structural alternatives were under consideration.

Figure 1. Photographs showing the forebay and water passage structures at Cougar Dam, Oregon. Left photograph shows the earthen dam, the cul-de-sac, and the temperature control tower at the eastern end of the dam. Right photograph shows the spillway Tainter gates at the western side of the dam. Photographs by John Beeman, U.S. Geological Survey, November 16, 2010, during a reservoir elevation of 1,580 ft National Geodetic Vertical Datum of 1929.

The 2008 Willamette Biological Opinion requires improvements to operations or structures to reduce impacts on Upper Willamette River (UWR) Chinook salmon (*Oncorhynchus tshawytscha*) and UWR steelhead (*Oncorhynchus mykiss*) (National Oceanic and Atmospheric Administration, 2008). The Opinion includes a requirement to install fish passage facilities (or operational alternatives) at Cougar Dam by 2014, if studies show that installation is feasible.

The study summarized in this report was designed to quantify juvenile Chinook salmon behavior in the reservoir and near the temperature control tower to help understand their spatial and temporal movements in those areas. Juvenile Chinook salmon, implanted with acoustic transmitters with an expected life of 91 d, were the basis for inference. The study was designed to collect data from fish released in March, April, and May, September, October, and November 2011 to address the following four objectives:

1. Determine if juvenile Chinook salmon of hatchery origin can be used as surrogates for naturally produced juvenile Chinook salmon.

2. Determine the spatial and temporal distribution of juvenile Chinook salmon in the Cougar Dam forebay near the temperature control tower.

3. Determine the spatial and temporal movements of juvenile Chinook salmon throughout the reservoir.

4. Capture fish from within Cougar Reservoir for species validation to aid a planned active hydroacoustic survey by Pacific Northwest National Laboratory.

This report is the second to describe data from juvenile salmonids implanted with acoustic transmitters in Cougar Reservoir. Beeman and others (2012) summarized preliminary results from the fish released during March, April, and May 2011. This report describes results from all fish released in 2011 and addresses objectives 1, 2, and 3. Results from objective 4 will be delivered by Pacific Northwest National Laboratory.

Methods

Fish Capture, Handling, Tagging, and Release

The data described in this report were collected from yearling (tagged in spring) and subyearling (tagged in fall) juvenile Chinook salmon tagged with acoustic transmitters and passive integrated transponder (PIT) tags. The tagged fish included those of hatchery and wild origins. Hatchery-origin fish were from the McKenzie River Hatchery in Leaburg, Oregon, and wild-origin fish were collected from within Cougar Reservoir.

In February and August 2011, about 650 and 1,000 hatchery fish, respectively, were sorted by size at McKenzie River Hatchery and placed in one-half of a full-length raceway to meet a minimum fork length requirement of 95 mm. The raceway was supplied with flowing river water. On 1 or 2 d every other week in March, April, May, September, October, and November, fish were netted from the raceway and placed into a 264-L transport tank and taken to the tagging site at the Cougar Dam adult fish facility, where they were held prior to tagging. The recommendations from the Surgical Protocols Steering Committee (2011) were followed in all aspects of the fish holding, tagging, and releasing procedures.

Wild fish were captured using a Lampara seine and an Oneida Lake trap. The Lampara seine was 91.4 m long and fished to a depth of about 7.6 m. The Lampara seine was fished by deploying the net from a boat, encircling an area, and then hauling the net back onto the boat deck. The Oneida Lake trap net, operated by the Oregon Department of Fish and Wildlife, is a passive capture method, and was constructed from 0.64-cm mesh and consisted of a 2.4-m^3 holding box, with a 3.4-m × 3.0-m lead net, and two 7.2-m × 3.0-m wings. The net generally is set near the shore, and anchored to stabilize it from wind and wave action. All fish collected were held in an aerated container supplied with fresh reservoir water, and then transported to the Cougar Dam adult fish facility and treated in the same manner as the hatchery fish.

Transmitter implantation and fish recovery were completed at the Cougar Dam adult fish facility. Fish were considered suitable for tagging if they were free of major injuries, had no external signs of gas bubble trauma or fungus, were less than or equal to 20 percent descaled, and were not previously tagged with acoustic PIT tags. To implant the transmitter, fish were anesthetized using buffered tricane methanesulfonate (MS-222, Argent Chemical Laboratories, Redmond, Washington) at a concentration of 75–80 mg/L. Fish weight and length were measured immediately prior to the surgery. Transmitters were those of the Juvenile Salmon Acoustic Telemetry System design (JSATS; McMichael and others, 2010), and were procured by the COE. Lotek Wireless (Newmarket, Ontario, Canada) provided the transmitters for the spring and Advanced Telemetry Systems (Isanti, Minnesota) provided the transmitters for the fall. The acoustic transmitters were 12 mm high × 5 mm wide × 4 mm deep, had an average mass of 0.43 g in air (0.42 g in spring, 0.44 g in fall), and had a volume of 0.14 mL. Expected transmitter life at the nominal pulse rate interval of 17 s was about 3 months (see section, "Transmitter Extinction Tests," for empirical measurement). A 23-mm-long PIT tag weighing 0.10 g was placed inside the body cavity along with the acoustic transmitter. All weighing, measuring, and containment equipment were treated with a 0.25 mL/L concentration of Stress Coat® (Aquarium Pharmaceuticals, Inc., Chalfont, Pennsylvania) to reduce handling-related stress to the fish via electrolyte loss. Fish were placed in a 19 L perforated recovery bucket filled with 7 L of river water immediately after surgery. Dissolved oxygen concentrations were maintained between 80 and 100 percent of saturation during recovery. Each recovery bucket held up to three fish. Fish were watched periodically during the first 10 min after surgery to ensure they recovered from anesthesia. Recovery buckets were then fitted with lids and placed in a raceway provided with flowing river water, where fish were held prior to release. The recovery buckets were floated in the raceway using rubber inner tubes around the top to allow fish access to air to adjust their buoyancy.

Tagged fish were released near the head of Cougar Reservoir. After the recovery period, fish were taken by boat upstream through Cougar Reservoir to the release site about halfway between the two shorelines near the Slide Creek boat ramp (fig. 2). Recovery buckets were removed from the raceway, inspected for mortalities, and transferred to an insulated 1,556-L plastic tank. Two tanks were mounted on a flatbed trailer with lids to limit water spillage during transport. Each tank was filled with river water and the fish were driven about 11.4 km to the boat ramp. Recovery buckets were then transferred onto a boat and taken upstream about 7.0 river kilometers to the release site. Water-quality measurements were recorded to ensure the water temperature difference between the recovery bucket and the reservoir was not greater than 2 C, which would require tempering in accordance with the Surgical Protocols Steering Committee (2011). Fish were released by partially submerging the buckets in the reservoir and gently tipping them over so the fish could swim out.

USGS High Resolution State Orthoimagery for Oregon, 2005, 0.5 meter resolution

Figure 2. Orthoimage showing locations of zones bounded by arrays of autonomous acoustic receivers (yellow circles) deployed in Cougar Reservoir, Oregon, 2011. The release location is indicated with a white arrow.

Reservoir Vertical Water Temperature Profile

We measured vertical water temperature profiles periodically near the log boom at the boat-restricted zone line and near the fish release site. Measurements were recorded on 11 dates between April 6, 2011, and February 7, 2012, near the boat-restricted zone line and on nine dates between May 5, 2011, and February 7, 2012, near the release site. Measurements were recorded by slowly lowering (about 0.5 m/s) a continuously recording bathythermograph (Model OS 200, Ocean Sensors, Inc.©, San Diego, California) from the reservoir surface to the bottom. Reservoir depths were recorded in feet following local convention. Water temperatures also are recorded hourly by the U.S. Army Corps of Engineers at about 3-m intervals using an automated series of thermistors at the northeastern corner of the temperature control tower.

Acoustic Telemetry Detection Systems

Signals from acoustic transmitters were detected using two types of JSATS hydrophone systems provided by the COE. The JSATS hydrophone systems were similar to those described by Weiland and others (2011). Deng and others (2011) described performance of the system for fish tracking in the Columbia River, and McMichael and others (2010) provides a general system description. Acoustic signals from tagged fish in the reservoir from approximately the log boom at the boat-restricted zone upstream to the head of the reservoir were detected using autonomous hydrophones spaced across the reservoir width at six locations (fig. 2). These hydrophones operate independently and record the presence of a transmitter when it is in range. We empirically determined that in the eastern arm of the reservoir, 82 percent of the expected number of transmissions were detected at a range of 105 m, and 10 percent were detected at a range of 180 m. Based on that data, the hydrophones were spaced about 100 m from shorelines and 200 m from each other at a depth of no more than about 33 mm from the water surface along lines across the reservoir (hereafter called "arrays"). Hydrophone depths were readjusted during bi-weekly visits to change batteries and download data. Several hydrophones were moored at depths greater than 33 mm from the water surface during March 2011. Hydrophones were deployed with steel anchors and float lines until April 2011, when they were deployed using a system of anchors and acoustic releases similar to those described by Titzler and others (2010), except that we used burlap bags of sand as anchors. The entire suite of 16 autonomous hydrophones was operational beginning on March 10, 2011.

Acoustic signals from tagged fish near the temperature control tower were detected using three 4-hydrophone systems linked to each other using a common clock. Each of these systems included four hydrophones connected with cables to a common computer. Each computer received its system time from a global positioning system. The use of a common time for all hydrophones allows estimation of fish position based on time of signal arrival if hydrophone locations and the speed of sound in the study area are known. The study was designed to use a laser-based system of estimating hydrophone positions, but purchasing delays required the use of a global positioning system-based method, which was installed on April 21, 2011, at 4 p.m. A similar cabled hydrophone system is described by Weiland and others (2009).

The cabled hydrophone systems were installed on the temperature control tower at several elevations and from floating platforms (figs. 3 and 4). The hydrophones at the lowest two elevations were installed beginning in January and became operational on March 17, 2011, after cables to connect them to the computers were delivered. The remaining cabled hydrophones became operational as the water elevation increased to the planned installation elevation (for hydrophones affixed to the tower) or as equipment became available (for hydrophones deployed from floating platforms). The eight hydrophones nearest the tower were all operational by April 5, 2011, and the entire system of cabled hydrophones was operational on April 21, 2011. Data prior to the installation of the hydrophone positioning system (April 21, 2011) is suitable for analyses based on the presence or absence of tagged fish, but cannot be used for estimating fish positions. The range of the cabled hydrophone systems was assumed to be similar to that of the autonomous hydrophones. This assumption seems reasonable because each transmitter message typically was detected by nearly all hydrophones, which were spaced about 80 m apart.

Figure 3. Photographs showing locations of cabled hydrophones nearest the temperature control tower at Cougar Dam, Oregon, 2011. Round symbols represent hydrophones affixed to the tower, and square symbols indicate those mounted from floating platforms. Numbers are hydrophone elevations. Dotted lines represent approximate locations of full and minimum conservation pool water elevations of 515 and 468 meters. Photograph during construction in 2005 provided by U.S. Army Corps of Engineers, and inset photographs taken by Amy Hansen and Scott Evans of the U.S. Geological Survey.

Fish positions used in this report were estimated using software developed through a subcontract as part of this study. The software program assumes a constant speed of sound and can estimate fish positions based on any of the hydrophones at which a transmitter message is detected. At the time of this report, the program was being developed further to include a graphical user interface and documentation, and to enable corrections to the speed of sound based on gradients in the study-area water temperature.

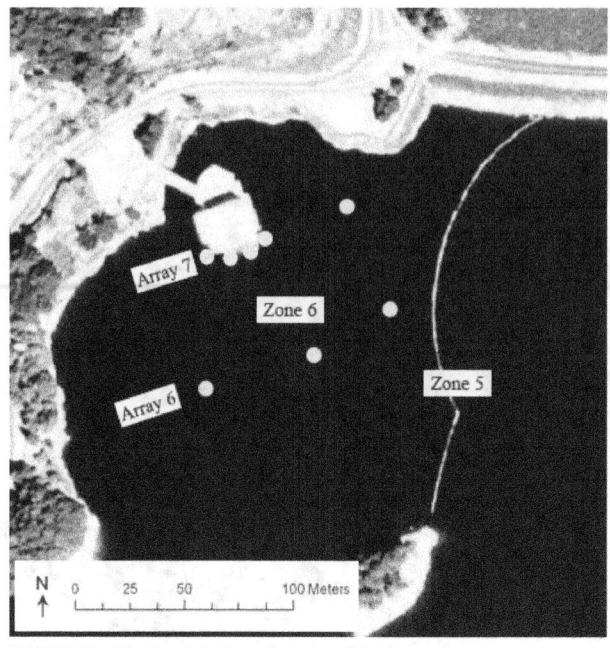

USGS High Resolution State Orthoimagery for Oregon, 2005, 0.5 meter resolution

Figure 4. Orthoimage showing locations of hydrophones deployed from floating platforms near the temperature control tower at Cougar Dam, Oregon, 2011. Array 7 hydrophones also are represented in figure 3.

Data Management and Analysis

Removing False-Positive Records

Data from the hydrophones were processed to remove false-positive records prior to analysis. False-positive records are those that indicate detection of a transmitter when the transmitter was not present, and are common in active telemetry systems. We used the procedures developed by Pacific Northwest National Laboratory (Mark Weiland, written commun., June 17, 2010) to remove false-positive records. The steps include removing records from tag codes not released, records suspected of being from reflections of valid tag signals (multipath), and records that are not close to a multiple of the tag pulse interval (McMichael and others, 2010). Records from the cabled hydrophone system also were required to be present on more than one hydrophone to be retained.

A series of zones were defined to enable analysis of fish movements. Zones were bounded by arrays in the reservoir, or by concentric rings specific distances from the temperature control tower (figs. 2, 4, and 5). General fish movements between arrays over time were plotted as an example of the raw data used in subsequent analyses. Analyses of fish presence (probability of presence at each array and across all arrays between release and the temperature control tower) and movement probabilities (Markov movement probabilities) were based on detections of fish at the arrays. The zones near the temperature control tower were bounded at 20-m intervals from the two zones nearest to the tower, which were within 15 and 5 m of the tower. These data were used in regressions described in the section, "Movements within the Reservoir and Dam Passage."

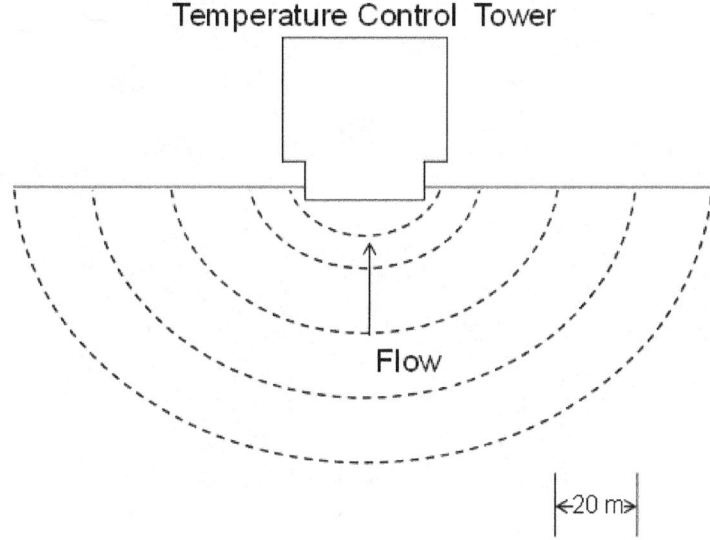

Temperature Control Tower

Flow

|←20 m→|

Figure 5. Diagram of zones used in analyses of data based on three-dimensional position estimates of fish near the temperature control tower at Cougar Dam, Oregon. The areas bounded by the dotted lines (from bottom up) are 75, 55, 35, 15, and 5 meters from the upstream face of the temperature control tower at Cougar Dam.

Movements within the Reservoir and Dam Passage

Descriptions of fish behavior and an analysis of factors affecting rates of movement in the reservoir and rate of dam passage were based on a select group of data. Considering that water temperature, discharge, and forebay elevation generally were not experimentally controlled, we based analyses of fish movements on data within narrow ranges of discharge that occurred at low and high reservoir elevations. This approach was used to analyze downstream movements of fish from reservoir zones 3 and 5, and dam passage from the zones bounded by the area near the temperature control tower with 3-dimensional fish positions. The ranges of data for each analysis were chosen after data were plotted with the appropriate events (downstream movement or dam passage) for discharge and elevation and ranges of discharge were selected that were present at low and high elevations. Given that the type of event and areas differed between analyses, the ranges of discharge and elevation differed slightly between the datasets used for each analysis. Data used for analysis of downstream movements included discharge ranges of 900–1,090 ft^3/s (low) and 1,500–1,690 ft^3/s (high), elevation ranges of 1,540.0–1,569.9 ft (low) and 1,664.3–1,689.9 ft (high), and data from 551 hatchery fish and 82 wild fish. Data used for analysis of dam passage included discharge ranges of 800–1,190 ft^3/s (low) and 1,410–1,800 ft^3/s (high), elevation ranges of 1,545.0–1,583.9 ft (low) and 1,670.0–1,689.9 ft (high), and data from 365–488 hatchery fish and 60–79 wild fish, depending on distance from the dam. Each analysis included the primary effects of fish origin (0 hatchery, 1 wild), elevation level (0 low, 1 high), discharge level (0 low, 1 high), and diel period (0 day, 1 night), as well as all possible two-way interactions. Cox-proportional hazards regression was used to estimate the effects of the independent variables on the dependent variable (rate of downstream movement or rate of dam passage). Variables were removed sequentially from the full model in decreasing order of the probability (P) of a greater Chi-Square value until all remaining variables were significant at $\alpha = 0.05$ level.

Dam passage was determined using presence data from the cabled hydrophones nearest the temperature control tower. The date and time of assumed dam passage were assigned if the first detection of the last transmitted message was at any of the four hydrophones located on the temperature control tower that were closest to the water surface. This method was chosen to limit passage assignments to fish last detected in the area generally between the water surface and the top of the weir gates, and was consistent with histories of tagged fish known to have passed the dam based on PIT-tag detections downstream.

Analyses of the timing and rates of downstream movement in the reservoir and dam passage were conducted using time-to-event methods (Hosmer and Lemeshow, 1999). These methods are ideally suited to analysis of data based on the timing of events, such as travel times, and the rates of event occurrences, such as the guidance, attraction, and passage of fish (Castro-Santos and Haro, 2010).

The time elapsed from fish release to two event types was described using Kaplan-Meier survivorship functions. The events are (1) detection by the cabled hydrophones mounted to the temperature control tower and the two hydrophones mounted on barges directly adjacent the tower, and (2) dam passage. The survivorship function of a variable T is defined as

$$S(t) = \Pr\{T > t\} \tag{1}$$

where T is a random variable with a probability distribution, denoting an event time for an individual. If the event of interest is passing a dam, the survivorship function gives the probability of not passing the dam after time t. As such, the median time occurs when the survivorship function equals 0.5. In the absence of censoring, the survivorship function represents the proportion of the population that has not experienced an event (for example, passing the dam). Examining the survivorship function can be useful to describe the timing of events as well as the proportion of the population still at risk of the event at different points in time. Fish that had not experienced an event by the longest known transmitter life were right censored at that time.

Cox proportional-hazards regression was used to determine the potential effects of dam discharge and diurnal period on the rates of dam passage. In Cox proportional-hazards regression, the rates of events are expressed as a hazard function defined as

$$h(t) = \lim_{\Delta t \to 0} \Pr\{t \leq T < t + 1 \mid T \geq t\} / \Delta t \tag{2}$$

representing the instantaneous risk, or rate, of an event occurring at time t. Equation 2 describes a conditional rate: It is the probability of the event occurring in a limited time interval, conditional on the event having not occurred yet, divided by the length of the interval (which makes it a rate, not a probability) (Allison, 1995). Results are expressed in terms of a hazard ratio that describes the change in the rate of interest for each unit increase in an independent variable. For continuous variables, the hazard rate is interpreted by subtracting 1 from the hazard ratio and multiplying the remainder by 100 percent. For dichotomous variables, the hazard ratio is interpreted directly. For example, a hazard ratio of 1.15 from a continuous covariate indicates that the rate of the event increases 15 percent for each unit increase in the covariate, and a hazard rate of 0.75 indicates a decrease of 25 percent per unit increase in the covariate. A hazard ratio of 2.00 for a dichotomous covariate (for example, day = 0, night = 1) indicates that the rate of the event is twice the value at the higher value relative to the lower value (at night compared to during the day in this example). Hazards are independent of the size of the population. The measure of interest generally is the hazard ratio, which is the ratio of the rate of an event relative to the values of a covariate (for example, day versus night). Hazard ratios of variables that are not involved in an interaction with one or more other variables can be read directly from most statistical package outputs, as listed in tables of section, "Results." However, hazard ratios of variables involved in interactions must be estimated from the parameter estimates (slopes) of each variable involved in the interaction plus their interaction term or terms.

The counting-process-style data input was used to divide the data into diel period (day or night) and to increment other time-varying covariates by hour (Hosmer and Lemeshow, 1999). We reset the time interval each time an individual entered a new zone or when it passed the dam. Censor variables of 0 (no event), 1 (downstream movement or dam passage), 2 (upstream movement), or 4 (end of expected tag life) were used in a competing risks analysis focusing on dam passage. We used the 90th percentile of expected tag life based on the spring transmitter extinction test (66 d) to censor the data from fish released in spring 2011, and 129 d to censor the data from fish released in fall 2011. The transmitters used in the spring and fall were from different manufacturers, but had similar pulse rates.

Movement Probabilities within the Reservoir

The probabilities of upstream and downstream movements at each array were estimated to determine if there were net upstream or downstream movements of fish and if the movements in the reservoir depended on past movements. Transition (movement) probabilities can be used to stochastically predict or simulate future fish movements (Johnson and others, 2004). A Markov-chain analysis was used to determine if movements between reservoir arrays followed a one-step process, by which movement from one array to an adjacent array is not dependent on its previous movement (a first-order Markov process; Bhat and Miller, 2002). We estimated the probability of a fish moving from one array to the next as either a first-order, or one-step process (not dependent on previous location) or a second order, or two-step process (dependent on previous location), and assessed support of the hypotheses by the data using the Akaike Information Criterion (Burnham and Anderson, 2002). The time of detection at each hydrophone array was used as an indicator of the timing of fish movements throughout the reservoir. The times used for this indicator were the first times of detection at any hydrophone within an array after previous detection at another array.

Probability of Presence near the Temperature Control Tower

We estimated the probability that a fish was present at least once after release at each array or at the temperature control tower. The purpose of this was to determine if fish near the head of the reservoir would be available for capture by a juvenile fish collection facility if one were present. This analysis does not indicate if fish that were not detected at an array or near the tower were alive or dead, only that they were never detected in the area of interest. The data were based on presence or absence of fish detected at the arrays throughout the reservoir or at the cabled hydrophone systems near the tower, which together detect fish within about 200 m of the tower.

The probability of being present near the temperature control tower at least once was estimated using Cormack-Jolly–Seber mark-recapture methodology (Cormack, 1964; Jolly, 1965; Seber, 1965) using Program MARK (White and Burnham, 1999). This method primarily is used to estimate survival and recapture probabilities in mark-recapture studies, but in this case we used it to estimate presence and recapture probabilities. Detection of a tagged animal is the joint probability of presence and being detected when present, so these parameters must be estimated separately. We constructed models of presence and recapture probabilities based on various hypotheses about differences between hatchery and wild fish and among arrays. In this analysis, the "recapture probability" at an array is the probability of being detected at that array at least once. Overdispersion in the data was estimated using the median $\hat{c}$ procedure in Program MARK. Models describing different hypotheses about processes driving presence or detection probabilities were evaluated using the Akaike Information Criterion with an adjustment for effects of sample size and overdispersion (QAICc). Burnham and Anderson (2002) suggest that when QAICc values differ by less than 2 units, the support for one hypothesis over another is not meaningfully different based on the data and models considered. However, one must cautiously evaluate models in this case to determine if the support of one of the models is simply because it is similar in structure to the other model. In such cases the difference in the number of parameters between the two models is 1 and the deviance or log-likelihood is essentially the same; the additional variable is sometimes called a "pretender" variable. They also suggest that QAICc differences of 4–7 indicate considerably less support for the model with the greater QAICc, and differences greater than 10 indicate essentially no support for the model with the greater QAICc. The probability of being present at the temperature control tower at least once was estimated as the product of array-specific presence probabilities, with the standard error (SE) estimated using the delta method (Seber, 1982). The probability of presence was estimated from model-averaged coefficients. A total of four models of recapture probabilities and five models of presence probabilities were considered based on various combinations of fish origin (hatchery or wild) and array.

Transmitter Extinction Tests

We selected 50 transmitters from the spring tags and 50 transmitters from the fall tags and empirically determined tag life. One of the spring tags was not operational so 49 tags in the spring and 50 tags in the fall were tested. In the spring, we activated the tags on May 20, 2011, placed them in 5-gallon (19 L) buckets and placed them in the Adult Fish Facility raceway where we held our fish during the post-surgery recovery. We used a Lotek model WHS 4000 JSATS acoustic receiver to detect tag signals. In the fall, we activated the tags on October 28, 2011, and placed them in a $3.25 \times 11.0 \times 1.25$ in. ($82.6 \times 279.4 \times 31.7$ mm) plastic box submerged in a 5 ft (1.5 m) diameter circular tank at the USGS Columbia River Research Laboratory in Cook, Washington and monitored with an Advanced Telemetry Systems model Trident SR5000 receiver where the hydrophone was placed in the tank and cabled to the receiver. The data was run through the same filter as the fish detection data and summarized with the time-to-event Kaplan-Meier survivorship analysis.

Results

Fish Capture, Handling, Tagging, and Release

A total of 415 hatchery fish and 29 wild fish were tagged and released from March 9, 2011, to May 20, 2011. The number of wild-origin fish collected was low with both gear types. Between March 7 and May 17, we completed 147 sets of the Lampara seine and collected 21 wild yearling Chinook salmon. The Oneida Lake trap net was fished for 26 d throughout the reservoir and collected 22 wild yearling Chinook salmon. The average size of tagged hatchery and wild fish was similar. The average fork lengths were 121.4 mm (range 98–152 mm) for hatchery fish and 120.6 mm (range 99–150 mm) for wild fish (table 1; note that one wild fish with a fork length of 215 mm was omitted from the size summary and analysis). The sizes of the wild fish from the two collection methods also were similar (table 2). The tag-weight-to-body-weight ratio based on the 0.53 g weight of the acoustic transmitter plus the PIT tag ranged from 1.6 to 6.0 percent with an average of 3.0 percent.

A total of 358 hatchery fish and 118 wild fish were tagged and released from September 8, 2011, to November 18, 2011. The collection of wild-origin fish was more effective than in the spring. Between September 20 and November 16, we completed 189 sets of the Lampara seine and collected approximately 400 wild subyearling Chinook salmon. The Oneida Lake trap net was fished for 25 d throughout the reservoir, and collected 260 wild subyearling Chinook salmon, 7 of which were transferred to U.S. Geological Survey. The average size of tagged hatchery and wild fish was similar. The average fork lengths were 122.8 mm (range 99–160 mm) for hatchery fish and 129.4 mm (range 97–207 mm) for wild fish (table 1). The sizes of the wild fish from the two collection methods also were similar (table 2). The tag-weight-to-body-weight ratio based on the 0.53 g weight of the acoustic transmitter plus the PIT tag ranged from 0.6 to 5.7 percent, with an average of 2.3 percent. Pre-tag holding times ranged from 17.3 to 25.5 h, and were within the 18–30 h specification of the Surgical Protocols Steering Committee (2011) in all but one instance where the time was 0.7 h shorter than the specification. Post-tag holding times ranged from 19.1 to 25.2 h in the spring and 17.9 to 25.6 h in the fall, and were within the 18–30 h specification in all but one case where the time was 0.1 h shorter than the specification.

Table 1. Summary statistics of fork length and weight of acoustic- and PIT-tagged hatchery and wild juvenile Chinook salmon, Cougar Reservoir, Oregon, 2011.

[N, number of fish collected; SD, standard deviation]

Fish origin	Fork length (millimeters)				Weight (grams)		
	N	Mean	SD	Range	Mean	SD	Range
Spring							
Hatchery	415	121.4	7.3	98–152	17.9	3.2	9.3–32.3
Wild	28	120.6	12.1	99–150	17.3	5.5	8.8–33.5
Fall							
Hatchery	358	122.8	14.4	99–160	21.6	7.3	10.8–43.1
Wild	118	129.4	15.2	97–207	24.6	10.1	9.3–93.3

Table 2. Summary statistics of fork length and weight by the different collection methods used to capture wild Chinook salmon, Cougar Reservoir, Oregon, 2011.

[N, number of fish collected; SD, standard deviation]

Collection method	Fork length (millimeters)				Weight (grams)		
	N	Mean	SD	Range	Mean	SD	Range
Spring							
Lampara seine	19	120.8	12.3	99–150	17.3	5.7	8.8–33.3
Oneida Lake trap	9	120.1	12.5	100–138	17.2	5.4	9.5–25.3
Fall							
Lampara seine	114	128.9	13.2	97–178	24.1	7.8	9.3–57.5
Oneida Lake trap	2	117.1	24.0	100–134	18.0	10.9	10.3–25.7
Hook and line	1	207.0			93.3		

No hatchery fish died in the spring or fall, but wild fish died during both tagging periods. During the spring, 10 of 43 wild fish collected (23 percent) died between collection and release. Several wild fish collected were not tagged. One spring fish captured in the Lampara seine was released prior to tagging. Seven fish from the Oneida Lake trap were not tagged; three were rejected based on condition and released alive, and four died before surgery. In the spring, there was a 5.0 percent (1 of 20) post-tagging mortality rate of fish collected in the Lampara seine and a 33.3 percent (5 of 15) post-tagging mortality rate of fish collected in the Oneida Lake trap. In the fall, 21 of 406 wild fish collected (5.2 percent) died between collection and release. Not all wild fish collected were tagged: 256 fish captured in the Lampara seine and 3 fish caught in the Oneida Lake trap were rejected based on quantity and condition and released alive. In the fall, there was a 10.2 percent (13 of 128) post-tagging mortality rate of fish collected in the Lampara seine, a 0 percent (0 of 2) post-tagging mortality rate of fish collected in the Oneida Lake trap, and a 100 percent (1 of 1) post-tagging mortality rate of fish collected with hook and line.

Many of the wild fish were infected by a parasitic copepod. A total of 31 of 41 spring wild fish examined had copepods present either on the gills (76 percent), at the insertion of the pectoral or pelvic fins, or a combination of these locations (table 3). One copepod was found on a hatchery fish prior to tagging (1 of 415; less than 1 percent). Samples of the copepods and seven of the mortalities with copepods were sent to the U.S. Fish and Wildlife Service, Lower Columbia River Fish Health Center, located in Willard, Washington. The copepods examined by U.S. Fish and Wildlife Service staff were consistent with the genus *Salmincola* (Mary Peters, U.S. Fish and Wildlife Service, written commun., 2011).

Most of the wild fall fish were infested with the parasitic copepod. Infection locations were on the pectoral or pelvic fins, gills, ventral side, or on the caudal peduncle with the bulk of the copepods on the pectoral and pelvic fins and gills. When we combined the copepod attachment location for all wild fish examined (number [N]=156), each fish had a mean of 3.2 copepods (standard deviation [SD] 2.9, range 0–22). The number of copepods was similar among sites, but was greatest in the gills.

Table 3. Summary statistics of number of copepods observed per wild Chinook salmon captured in Cougar Reservoir, Oregon, during the fall tagging season, 2011.

[N, number of fish; SD, standard deviation]

Group	N	Pectoral fins			Pelvic fins			Gills		
		Mean	SD	Range	Mean	SD	Range	Mean	SD	Range
All fall fish	156	1.1	1.0	0–5	1.1	0.4	0–2	1.7	1.4	0–13
Tagged and released	118	1.2	0.8	0–4	1.1	0.4	0–2	1.4	0.9	0–5
Tagged and mortality	13	1.1	0.9	0–3	1.0	0.0	1–1	1.8	1.2	0–4
Untagged	25	1.0	1.2	0–5	1.0	0.0	1–1	2.7	2.4	1–13

Several observations were omitted prior to analysis. One wild fish in the spring with a fork length of 215 mm was omitted because it was more than 50 mm larger than any other fish captured and was likely not in the same year class as the others. Data from three hatchery fish and one wild fish released in the spring and two hatchery fish and one wild fish released in the fall that were never detected after release were omitted. We omitted data from one wild fish and one hatchery fish that continuously travelled together in the spring near the temperature control tower and that were suspected of being eaten by a predator. The environmental data from the 7 a.m. hour on May 25 were omitted because the data indicated that the discharge was 4,100 ft^3/s, which was at least 1,560 ft^3/s greater than the discharge in the adjacent hours. After omitting these data, the analysis used 411 (415-4) hatchery fish and 26 (29-3) wild fish tagged in the spring, and 356 (358-2) hatchery fish and 117 (118-1) wild fish tagged in the fall.

Transmitter Extinction Tests

Tag lives were empirically determined to enable censoring of detection data when the probability of transmitter function was low. The median life of the spring tags tested was 110.7 d, and the maximum life was 127.5 d (fig. 6). The first tag stopped working after 27.5 d and many stopped working after about 60 d. The 90th percentile of tag life was 66 d. The median life of the fall tags tested was 139.6 d and the maximum life was 156.9 d. The first tag expired at 113.7 d and the 90th percentile of tag life was 129.0 d. To reduce the probability of false positive detections in the data, we truncated or censored each fish detection history at the 90th percentile of the empirically determined tag life. Four of the "spring" tags were used in the fall.

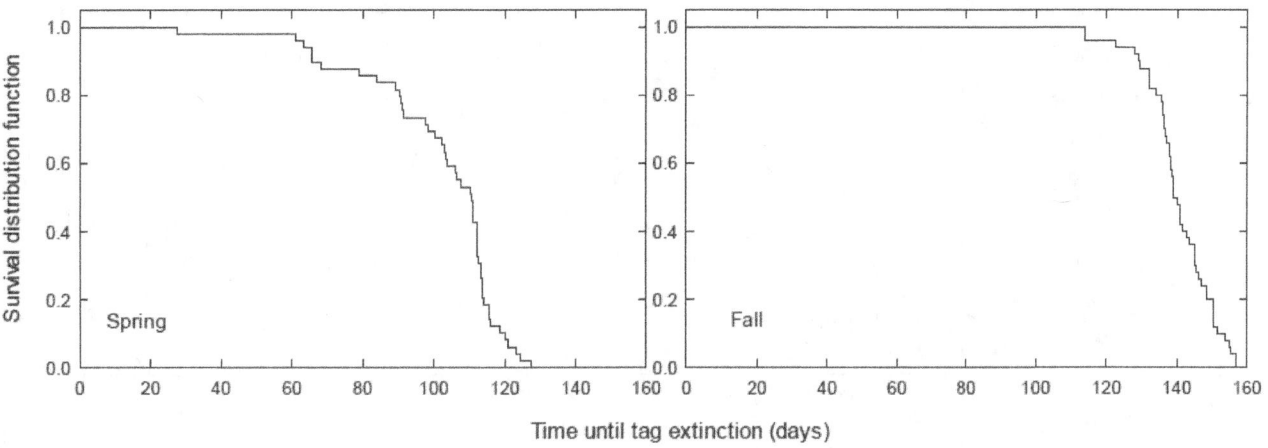

Figure 6. Graphs of survival distribution functions of time until extinction of transmitter models implanted in juvenile Chinook salmon released into Cougar Reservoir, Oregon, spring and fall 2011.

Definition of Spring and Fall Study Periods

Data from fish tagged during the spring and fall were often analyzed separately. Inasmuch as the transmitters used during this study were expected to function for about 3 months, the period of data collection from fish released spanned several months. Thus, based on the 90th percentile of tag lives empirically determined in the transmitter extinction tests, we define the "spring" analysis period from March 9, 2011, to July 24, 2011 inclusive and the "fall" analysis period from September 8, 2011, to February 27, 2012 inclusive. These periods will hereafter be referred to as the spring and fall periods.

Environmental Conditions and Dam Operations

Cougar Dam operation and environmental conditions varied throughout the year. We present daily mean data that are calculated from the mean hourly data. The mean hourly data vary more than the mean daily data presented here. During the spring period, the median daily powerhouse discharge was 526.3 ft³/s (range 0–950.0 ft³/s) and the median daily RO discharge was 724.6 ft³/s (range 0–2,062.9 ft³/s; fig. 7). The median daily reservoir elevation was 1,681.1 ft (range 1,580.6–1,689.9 ft) and the median temperature of the top 13–19 ft was 8.4 °C (range 4.5–15.7 °C). Temperature increased steadily until July 13 and then it ranged from 13.1 to 16.5 °C until the fall period. The median daily head (depth over the upper weir gates) was 14.5 ft (range 5.8–35.3 ft). Head followed discharge until July 1, after which it remained fairly constant through the remainder of the spring period.

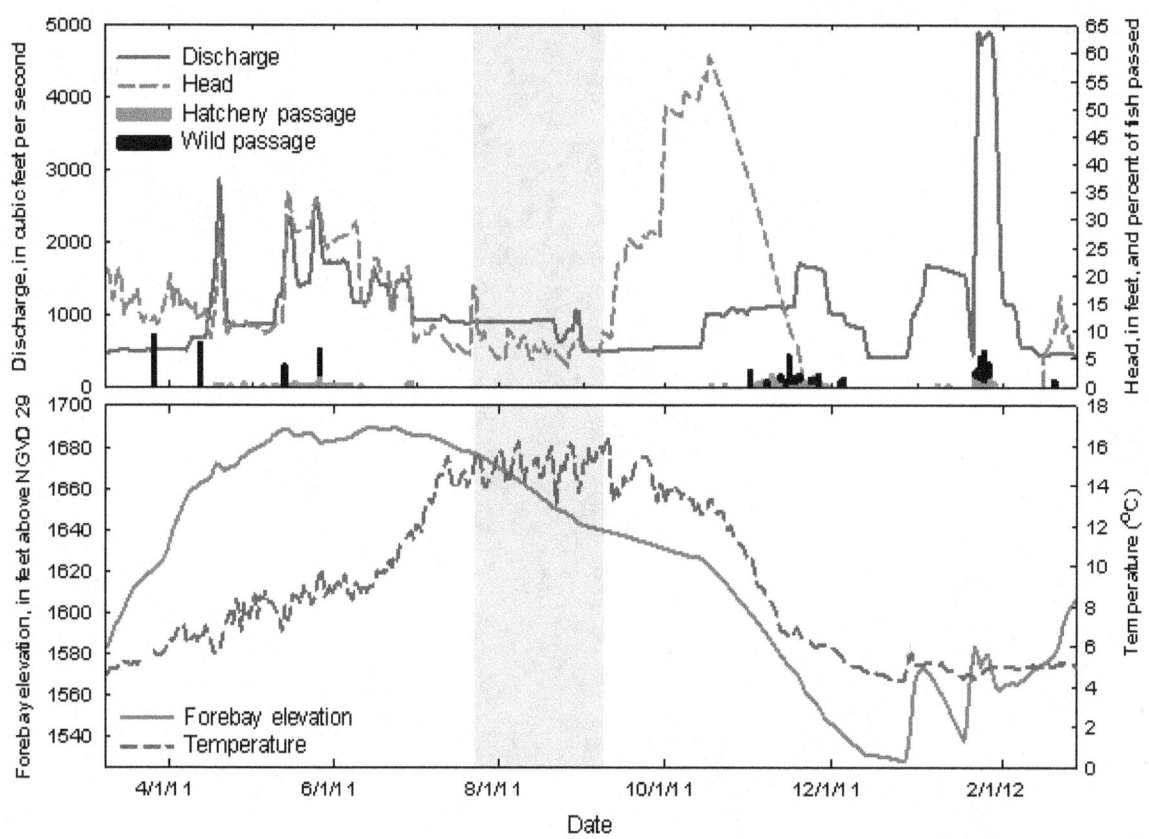

Figure 7. Graphs of total dam discharge and head above the weir gates (top), and forebay elevation and water temperature (bottom) at Cougar Dam, Oregon, 2011–12. Water temperature is the average of the upper 13–19 feet of the water column near the temperature control tower. Additionally, the top graph shows dates of dam passage of wild and hatchery fish as a percent of fish in the reservoir available to pass. Shaded area indicates periods likely without live tags in the reservoir (see fig. 9).

During the fall period, the temperature and reservoir elevation decreased and head and total discharge had sharp peaks (fig. 7). Median daily powerhouse discharge was 545.4 ft^3/s (range 301.7–1,241.7 ft^3/s) and median daily RO discharge was 0 ft^3/s (range 0–3,782.9 ft^3/s). Daily mean total discharge was between 500 and 1,585 ft^3/s through November 18, and then increased to 4,902.9 ft^3/s on January 27. Mean daily reservoir elevation decreased from September 8 through December 27 (when it was 1,527.7 ft), and then peaked twice in January. Median daily reservoir elevation was 1,574.5 ft (range 1,527.7–1,639.8 ft). Median daily temperature of the top 13–19 ft of the water column was 5.7 °C (range 4.3–16.5 °C), and decreased steadily until December 6. Mean daily head increased steadily in the beginning of the fall period until October 17, when there was a sharp decrease until the water elevation was below the lowest weir gate elevation (1,571 ft) on November 20. Median daily head was 28.9 ft and ranged from 2.0 to 59.6 ft. The weir gates were redeployed on February 16.

Vertical water temperature profiles at comparable depths were similar near the boat-restricted zone and near the release site (fig. 8). A thermocline was present between about 10 and 30 ft in depth, depending on the date. The water temperature profiles from the two sites in the reservoir generally were similar to the data from the sensors at the temperature control tower, though the warmest temperatures were at the release site.

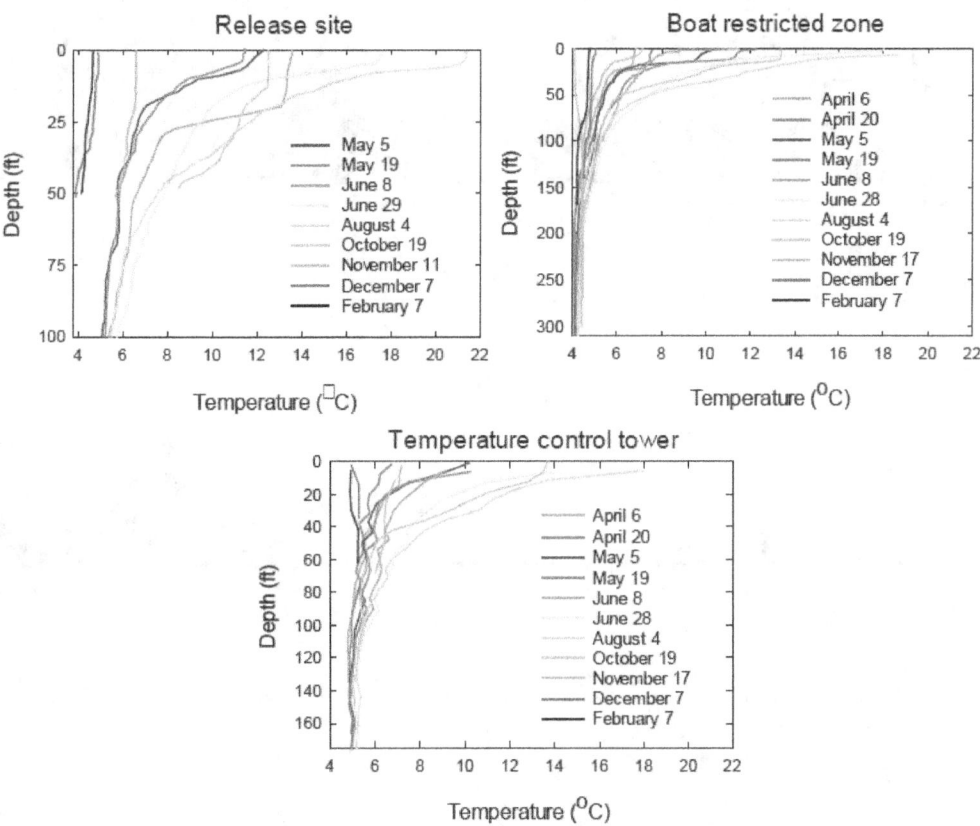

Figure 8. Vertical temperature profiles of Cougar Reservoir, Oregon, collected at the fish release site, near the boat-restricted zone boundary, and at the temperature control tower, April 6, 2011–February 7, 2012. Note the different y-axis scales.

Movements within the Reservoir

Movements within the reservoir are based primarily on detections of tagged fish at autonomous hydrophones placed throughout the reservoir. Movements of tagged fish are described in general terms, followed by more specific analyses of movements and factors affecting downstream movements, and finally estimates of fish positions near the temperature control tower. The release schedule and tag lives were sufficient to enable hatchery fish with live tags to be present nearly all year, but they were likely absent from July 25, 2011, to September 7, 2011 (fig. 9). Tagged wild fish were released over a smaller range of dates than hatchery fish, and tagged wild fish with live tags were likely absent from July 11, 2011, to September 8, 2011. There were few wild fish with live tags during the fall prior to October 8, 2011 (fig. 9).

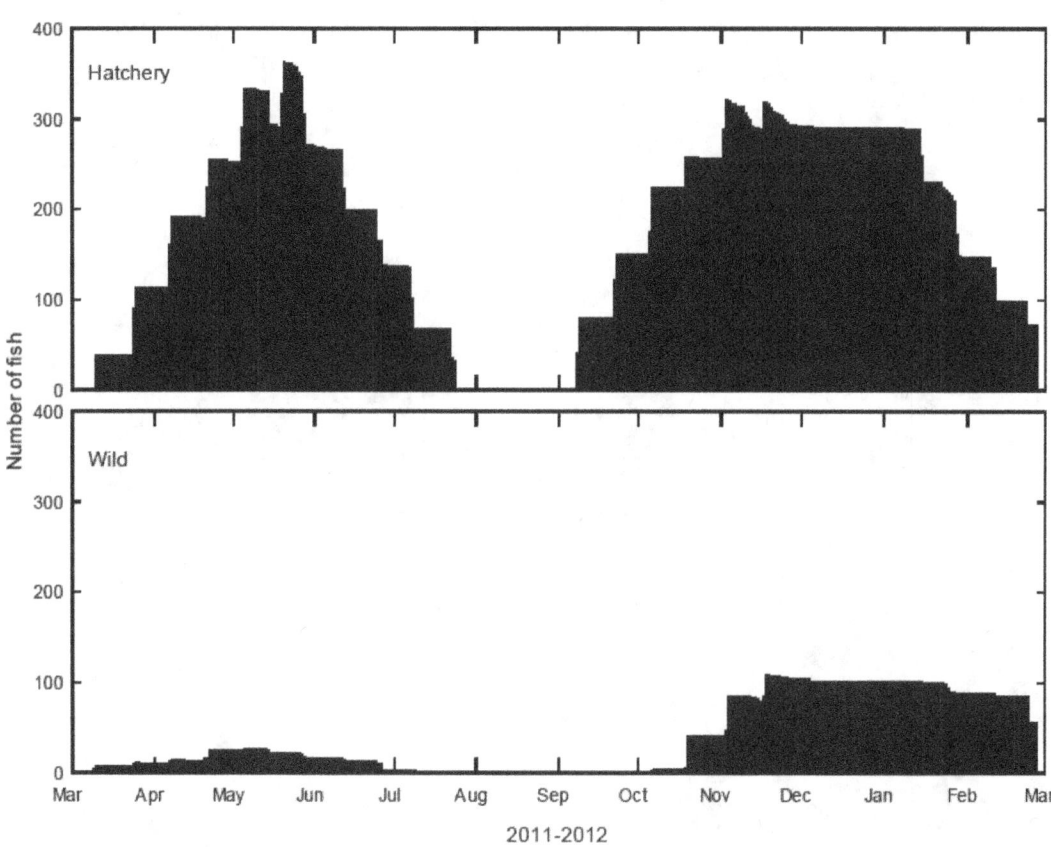

Figure 9. Graphs showing number of fish available to pass with live tags in Cougar Reservoir, Oregon, by fish origin, March 9, 2011–February 27, 2012.

General Fish Behavior

Most tagged fish moved throughout the reservoir, making repeated trips through most zones. Most tagged fish were detected in the area within about 100 m of the temperature control tower (zone 6) at least once. Graphs of general fish movements of several randomly selected hatchery and wild fish tagged in the spring and fall are shown in figures 10 and 11. A pattern of directed movements throughout the reservoir is evident in several of the graphs. It also is evident that the data from some fish ended prior to the expected life of the transmitter. A lack of detections often is assumed to be an indicator of mortality, but it also is possible the fish stopped moving between hydrophones, the fish continued to move undetected, or the transmitter stopped working prematurely. Of these possible explanations, the last two appear unlikely based on information about detection probabilities and transmitter reliability from the transmitter extinction tests.

Eighteen of the 26 wild fish released in the spring and used in analyses were detected in zone 6 at least once during the day, and 17 were detected at least once at night. During the day, they made 1–34 trips into zone 6 with an average of 8.4 trips per fish. At night, they made 1–35 trips into zone 6, with an average of 8.6 trips per fish. Many (334) of the 411 hatchery fish released in the spring and used in analyses were detected in zone 6 during the day, and 328 were detected there during the night. During the day, the hatchery fish made 1–80 trips into zone 6, with an average of 11.9 trips per fish. At night, they made 1–81 trips per fish, with an average of 11.2 per fish.

The fish tagged in the fall made fewer trips into zone 6 than those tagged in spring, which may be partly due to greater dam passage rates in the fall period compared to the spring period (see section, "Dam Passage"). A total of 75 of 117 wild fish released in the fall and used in analyses were detected in zone 6 during the day, and 83 were detected there at least once during the night. The wild fish made a fall period average of 4.2 trips into zone 6 during the day (range 1–18), and 4.5 trips during the night (range 1–20). A total of 257 of the 356 hatchery fish released in the fall and used in analyses were detected in zone 6 during the day, and 285 were detected there at night. The hatchery fish made a season-wide average of 11.2 trips into zone 6 in the day (range 1–44), and 10.9 trips there at night (range 1–45).

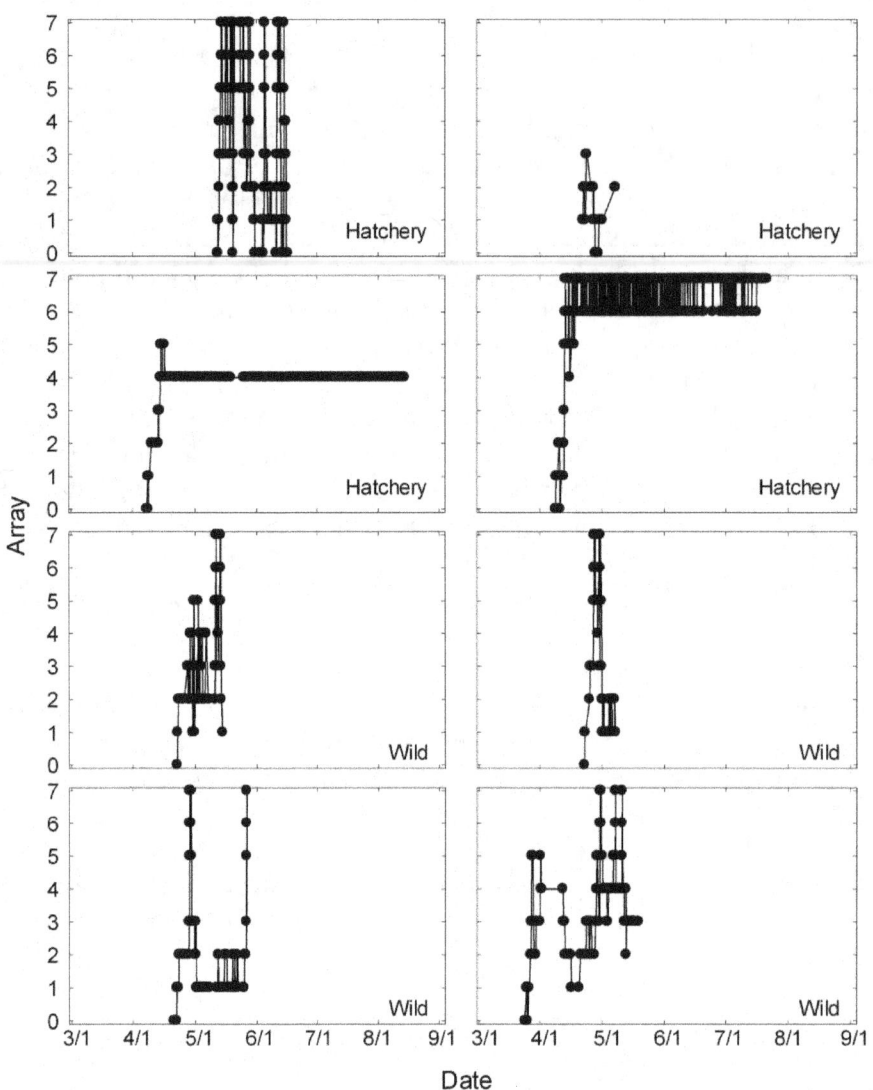

Figure 10. Graphs of movements of randomly selected juvenile Chinook salmon in Cougar Reservoir, Oregon, during the spring period 2011. Arrays 0–5 are autonomous nodes within the reservoir proper, array 6 is a cabled-node system about 100 meters from the temperature control tower, and array 7 is a cabled-node system affixed to the temperature control tower (see fig. 2 for schematic).

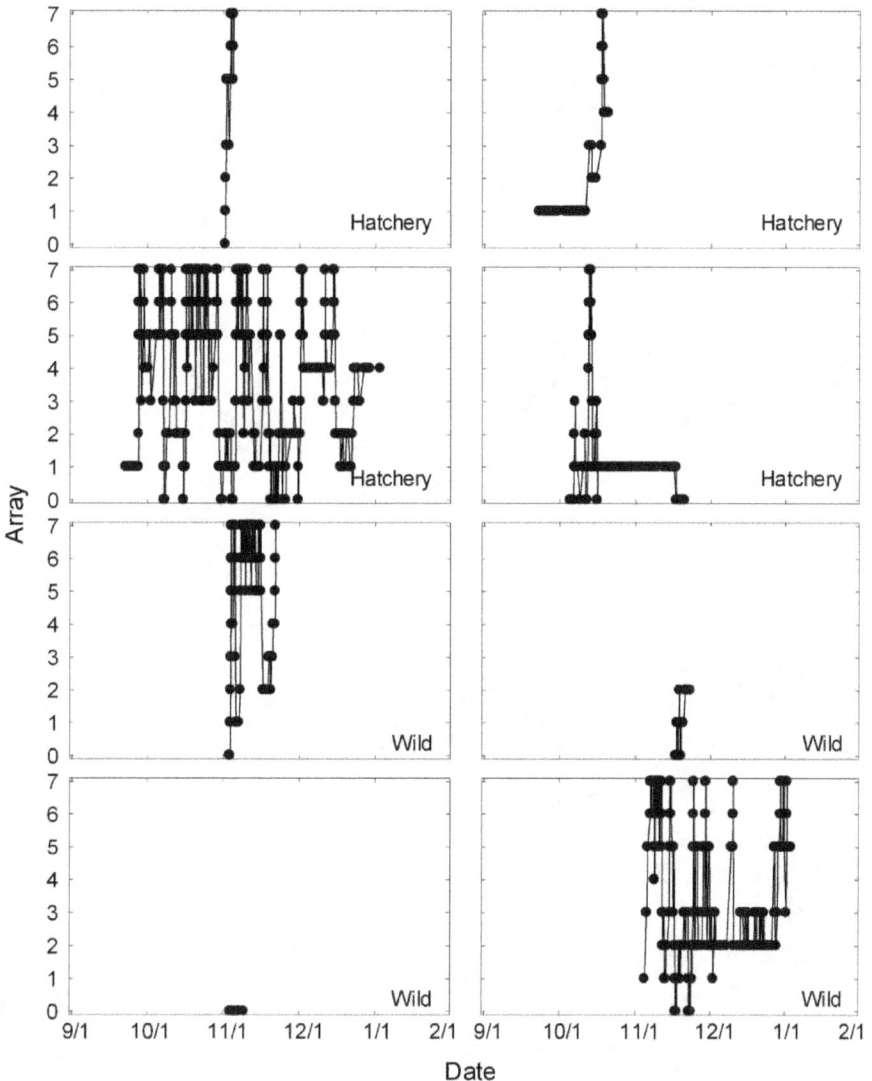

Figure 11. Graphs of movements of randomly selected juvenile Chinook salmon in Cougar Reservoir, Oregon, during the fall of 2011 and winter of 2012. Arrays 0–5 are autonomous nodes within the reservoir proper, array 6 is a cabled-node system about 100 meters from the temperature control tower, and array 7 is a cabled-node system affixed to the temperature control tower (see fig. 2 for schematic).

Timing of Detection

The hour of day when hatchery and wild fish were detected, an indicator of the timing of fish movements, differed between the spring and fall periods (fig. 12). During the spring period, the hour of detection for hatchery fish at most arrays was similarly distributed between the day and night hours. The only exception to this was at the eastern arm (array 4), where a peak of detections occurred at about dawn. The tagged wild fish movements in the spring period were widely distributed throughout the day as well, but showed considerable variation from hour to hour. During the fall period, hatchery and wild fish movements occurred more at night than during the day at all arrays. About 87 percent of the hatchery fish movements from array 5 to the temperature control tower were first detected at the tower from 5:00 p.m. to 7:59 a.m., and 13 percent occurred from 8:00 a.m. to 4:59 p.m. Similarly, 84 percent of the wild fish movements to the tower occurred from 5:00 p.m. to 7:59 a.m., and 16 percent occurred from 8:00 a.m. to 4:59 p.m.. A strong peak in hatchery and wild fish movements to the tower in the fall period occurred at about 6:00 a.m. to 7:00 a.m., while a peak in detections at array 5 from the adjacent arrays occurred from about 5:00 p.m. to 6:00 p.m..

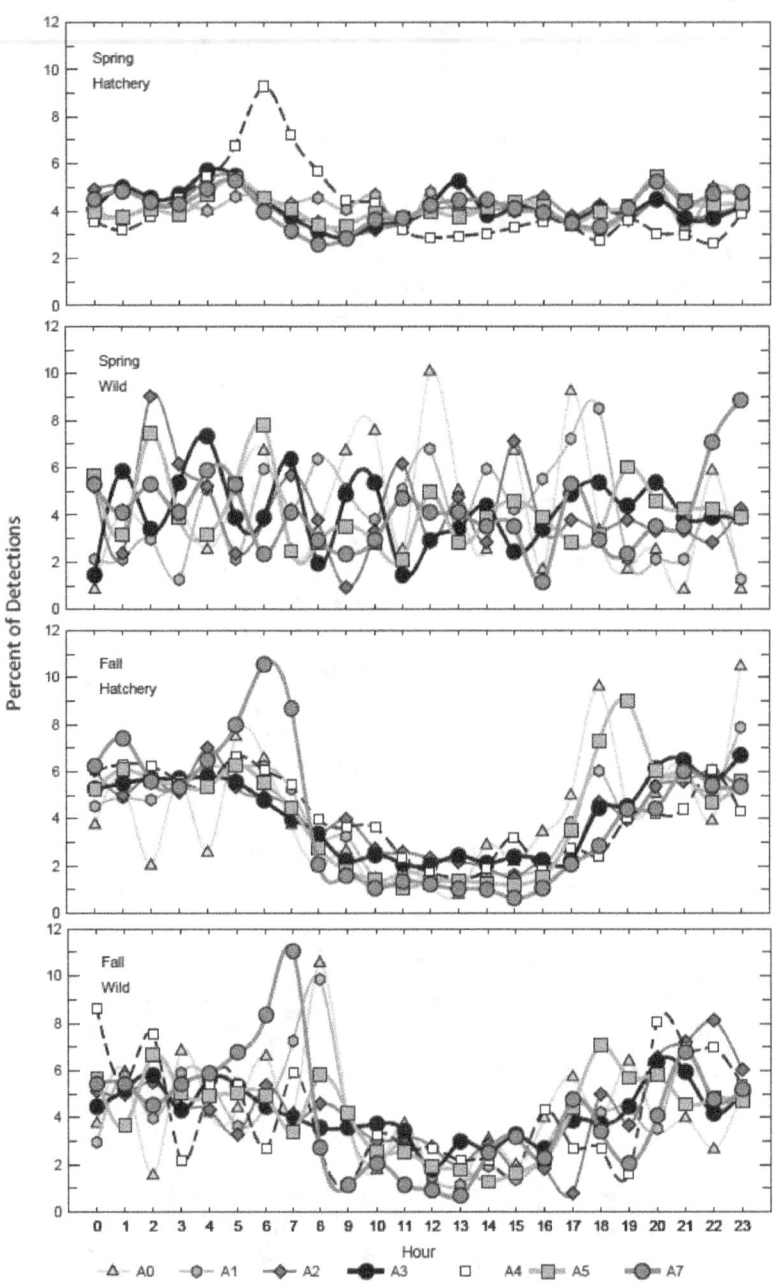

Figure 12. Graphs showing hour of detection of hatchery and wild Chinook salmon released into Cougar Reservoir, Oregon, spring and fall 2011, at arrays 0–7 (temperature control tower). A1–A7 indicate detection arrays 1–7.

Travel Time from Release to the Temperature Control Tower and to Dam Passage

During the spring period the travel times of hatchery and wild fish for the first trip from release to the temperature control tower were similar. Travel times ranged from 0.6 to 63.6 d for hatchery fish, and from 3.3 to 36.4 d for wild fish, with medians of 9.6 d and 9.1 d for hatchery and wild fish, respectively (fig. 13). A total of 335 hatchery fish and 18 wild fish tagged in the spring were detected near the temperature control tower.

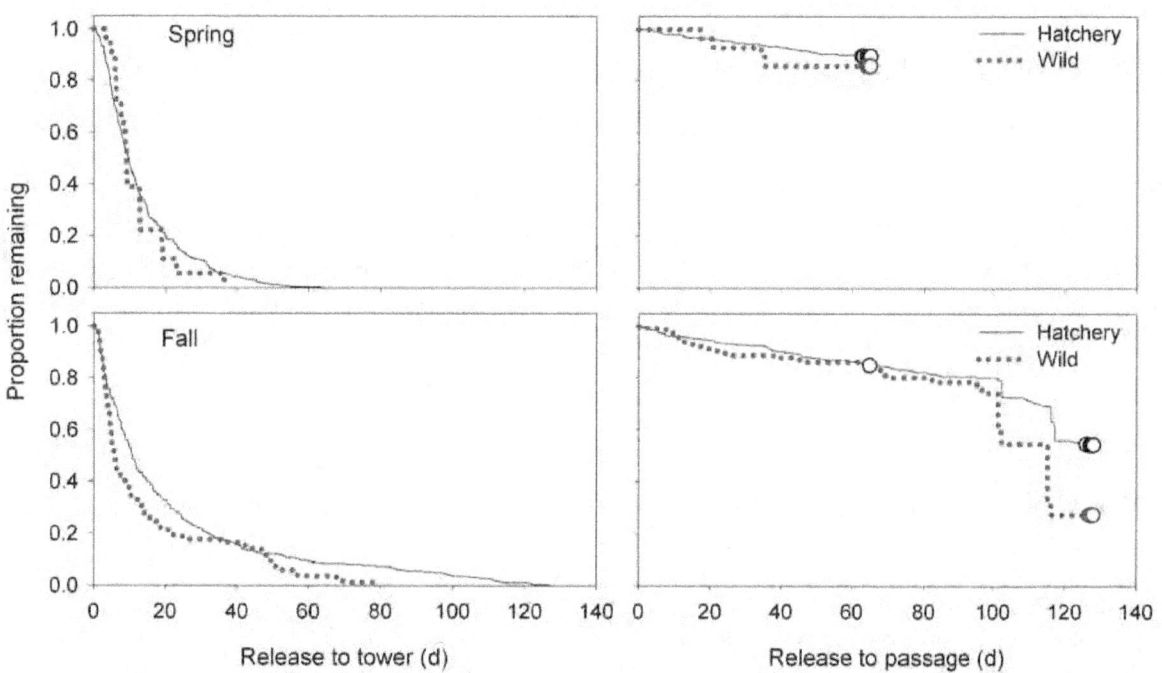

Figure 13. Time from release to first detection at the Cougar Dam temperature control tower (left graphs) and time from release to dam passage (right graphs) for hatchery (solid line) and wild (dotted line) juvenile Chinook salmon released into Cougar Reservoir, Oregon, spring and fall 2011. Open circles represent censored fish that did not pass before the end of the tag life. The last two releases in the fall only had 101 days and 115 days from release until the last day in study on February 27, 2012, instead of the 129 days of tag life allowed for the remainder of the fish.

The times from release to dam passage also were similar for hatchery and wild fish in the spring period. Time from release to dam passage ranged from 2.5 to 61.5 d for hatchery fish and from 17.2 to 35.4 d for wild fish (fig. 13). Median times from release to dam passage were not estimable because less than 50 percent of the fish in the reservoir passed within the expected tag life. A total of 43 hatchery fish and 4 wild fish were detected passing the dam during the expected tag life. Five additional hatchery fish and 2 wild fish were known to have passed the dam after the expected tag life.

During the fall period the travel times for the first trip from release to the temperature control tower followed a trend similar to that in the spring period. Travel times ranged from 0.5 to 126.3 d for hatchery fish and from 0.6 to 52.5 d for wild fish, with medians of 10.7 d and 5.7 d for hatchery and wild fish, respectively (fig. 13). A total of 291 hatchery and 85 wild fish were detected near the temperature control tower.

The times from release to dam passage also were similar for hatchery and wild fish in the fall period. Median times from release to dam passage were not estimable for hatchery fish because less than 50 percent of hatchery fish released passed the dam; however, the median time from release to dam passage was 115.2 d for wild fish (fig. 13). Time from release to dam passage ranged from 0.6 to 126.4 d for hatchery fish, and from 2.5 to 116.1 d for wild fish. A total of 89 hatchery fish and 30 wild fish were detected passing the dam during the expected tag life. One additional hatchery fish tagged in the fall is known to have passed the dam after the expected tag life. One hatchery fish tagged in the fall passed without detection, as indicated by detection at a downstream PIT system.

Probability of Presence near the Temperature Control Tower

The probabilities of presence at each array and at the temperature control tower were based on model-averaged estimates from a suite of models. There were a total of four models of presence probability for the spring period, and a total of five models for the fall period, each with a common model of detection probability (table 4). There was little evidence for fish origin effects on detection probabilities. The models with detection probabilities varying only among arrays received about 91 percent or more of the model weights (table 4). The detection probabilities ranged from 0.964 (SE 0.013) to 1.000 (SE 0.000) among arrays during the spring period, and from 0.946 (SE 0.018) to 1.000 (SE 0.000) among arrays during the fall period.

Table 4. Suite of models of detection probabilities for the analysis of presence probabilities of juvenile Chinook salmon released into Cougar Reservoir, Oregon, during spring and fall 2011.

[Models of detection probability (P) include combinations of fish origin (hatchery, wild), array, and a common value fitted to all combinations of origin and array (.). All models shared a common presence probability model of a multiplicative combination of origin and array. Num. par, number of parameters; +, an additive effect; Na, a model is not applicable because of removal from consideration owing to a "pretender" status. A $\hat{c}$ value of 1.891 was applied to the spring data, and a $\hat{c}$ value of 1.948 was applied to the fall data. QAIC and QDeviance are the Akaike Information Criterion and Deviance adjusted for overdispersion]

Model	QAICc	Delta QAICc	QAICc weights	Model likelihood	Num. par	QDeviance
------------ Spring ------------						
1 P(array)	459.613	0.000	0.907	1.000	9	16.825
2 P (origin+array)	459.896	0.283	Na	Na	10	15.091
3 P(.)	464.852	5.240	0.066	0.073	6	28.105
4 P(origin)	466.646	7.033	0.027	0.030	7	27.887
------------ Fall ------------						
1 P(array)	520.661	0.000	0.932	1.000	13	35.172
2 P(.)	525.893	5.232	0.068	0.073	10	46.462
3 P(origin)	527.817	7.156	Na	Na	11	46.369
4 P(origin+array)	1910.869	1390.208	0.000	0.000	13	1425.381
5 P (origin*array)	1914.175	1393.514	0.000	0.000	15	1424.640

The probability of being present at an array decreased as the distance from the release site increased, and estimates were higher for hatchery fish than for wild fish (fig. 14). However, the support was equivocal for models with and without differences in the probability of presence between hatchery and wild fish in the spring period. A difference in QAICc of about 1 between the model with origin and array factors (model 1) and the model without an origin factor (model 2) indicates that support for both models was nearly equal; the other models were unsupported (table 5). For the fall period, the difference in QAICc between the models with and without origin (models 1 and 3) was about 4, indicating considerably less support for the hypothesis of differences between hatchery and wild fish than the hypothesis of no difference based on fish origin (table 6). The estimated cumulative probability that a fish was present at the temperature control tower at least once during the spring period was 0.835 (SE 0.025) for hatchery fish and 0.743 (SE 0.089) for wild fish (fig. 14). During the fall period, the cumulative probability of presence was 0.841 (SE 0.026) for hatchery fish and 0.810 (SE 0.040) for wild fish.

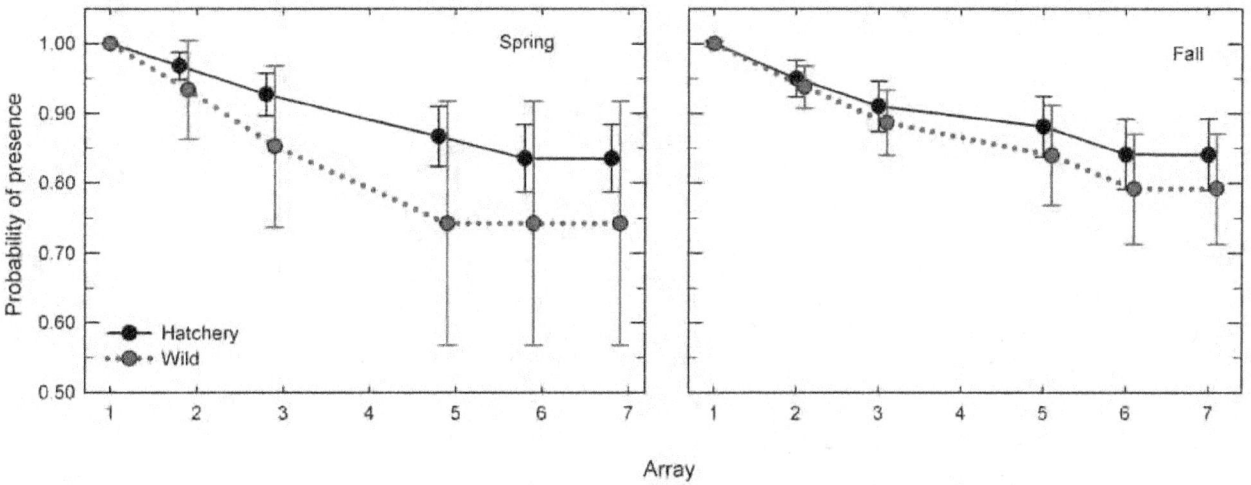

Figure 14. Graphs showing cumulative probabilities (± 95-percent confidence interval) of being present at least once at reservoir arrays 1, 2, 3, and 5, and at arrays 6 and 7 near the temperature control tower for fish released into Cougar Reservoir, Oregon, spring and fall 2011. Array 4 in the eastern arm of the reservoir was not used in this analysis because fish can migrate to the temperature control tower without entering that area.

Table 5. Suite of models used in estimation of presence probabilities of juvenile Chinook salmon released into Cougar Reservoir, Oregon, spring 2011.

[Models of presence probability (M) include combinations of fish origin (hatchery, wild), array, and a common value fitted to all combinations of origin and array (.). Num. par, number of parameters; +, an additive effect; *, a multiplicative effect. A ĉ value of 1.891 was applied to the data. QAIC and QDeviance are the Akaike Information Criterion and Deviance adjusted for overdispersion]

Model	QAICc	Delta QAICc	QAICc weights	Model likelihood	Num. par	QDeviance
1 M(origin+array), P (array)	459.613	0.000	0.628	1.000	9	16.825
2 M(array), P (array)	460.659	1.046	0.372	0.593	8	19.886
3 M(.), P (array)	477.684	18.071	0.000	0.000	5	42.947
4 M(origin), P (array)	477.859	18.2466	0.000	0.000	6	41.112

Table 6. Suite of models used in estimation of fall presence probabilities of juvenile Chinook salmon released into Cougar Reservoir, Oregon, fall 2011.

[Models of presence probability (M) include combinations of fish origin (hatchery, wild), array, and a common value fitted to all combinations of origin and array (.). Num. par, number of parameters; +, an additive effect; *, a multiplicative effect; Na, a model is not applicable because of removal from consideration owing to a "pretender" status. A ĉ value of 1.551 was applied to the data. QAIC and QDeviance are the Akaike Information Criterion and Deviance adjusted for overdispersion]

Model	QAICc	Delta QAICc	QAICc weights	Model likelihood	Num. par	QDeviance
1 M(array), P (array)	516.603	0.000	0.881	1.000	10	37.173
2 M(origin+array), P (array)	516.885	0.282	Na	Na	11	35.437
3 M(origin*array), P (array)	520.661	4.058	0.116	0.131	13	35.172
4 M(.), P (array)	529.117	12.514	0.002	0.002	6	57.742
5 M(origin), P (array)	529.291	12.688	0.002	0.002	7	55.904

Movement Probabilities within the Reservoir

Results of analyses of transition probabilities for hatchery and wild fish between arrays in the reservoir indicated fish movements most often were directionally persistent (figs. 15 and 16; appendix table A1). This means that fish detected at an array upstream of their last known location were more likely to continue swimming upstream to the next upstream array than they were likely to turn around and swim to the downstream array. Likewise, fish that had been previously moving downstream were more likely to continue moving downstream of the current detection array than they were likely to move upstream. Such movements are described by a two-step Markov chain, in which the probability of an individual moving from one location to an adjacent location depends on where it was previously located, as opposed to the simpler one-step Markov chain where the probability of moving from the current location to an adjacent location depends only on the individual's current location (that is, random movement).

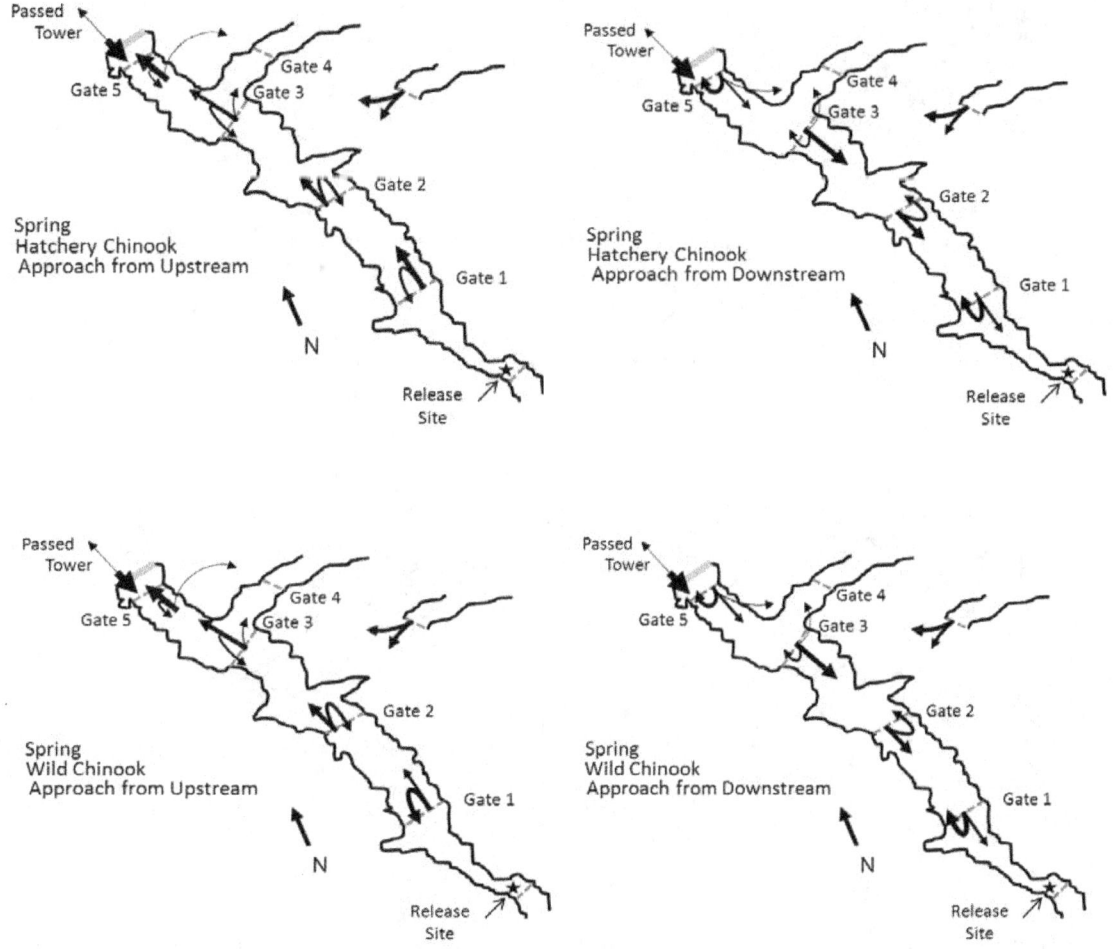

Figure 15. Transition probabilities of hatchery and wild fish released in Cougar Reservoir, Oregon, spring 2011. Relative width of arrows indicates probabilities of moving from one array to an adjacent array based on the previous movement (see appendix table A1 for probabilities). Transition probabilities at gates 3 and 5 do not include fish coming from gate 4; transitions from gate 4 are shown to the right of each diagram.

Transition probabilities of hatchery and wild fish were estimated for 24 combinations of movements between adjacent reservoir arrays. Models of two-step Markov chains were supported over those of one-step Markov chains in 30 of the 48 possible cases based on data from the spring period and in 35 of the 48 possible cases based on data from the fall period (appendix tables A2, A3). A specific example of this directional movement is demonstrated by the higher probability that both hatchery and wild fish moved downstream of array 1 to array 2 and then to array 3 (0.57–0.61), compared to the probability that fish moved downstream of array 1 to array 2 and then swam back upstream to array 1 (0.39–0.43; figs. 14 and 15; appendix table A1). For fish moving downstream, the probability that a fish continued to move downstream of its current location generally increased as it got closer to the dam.

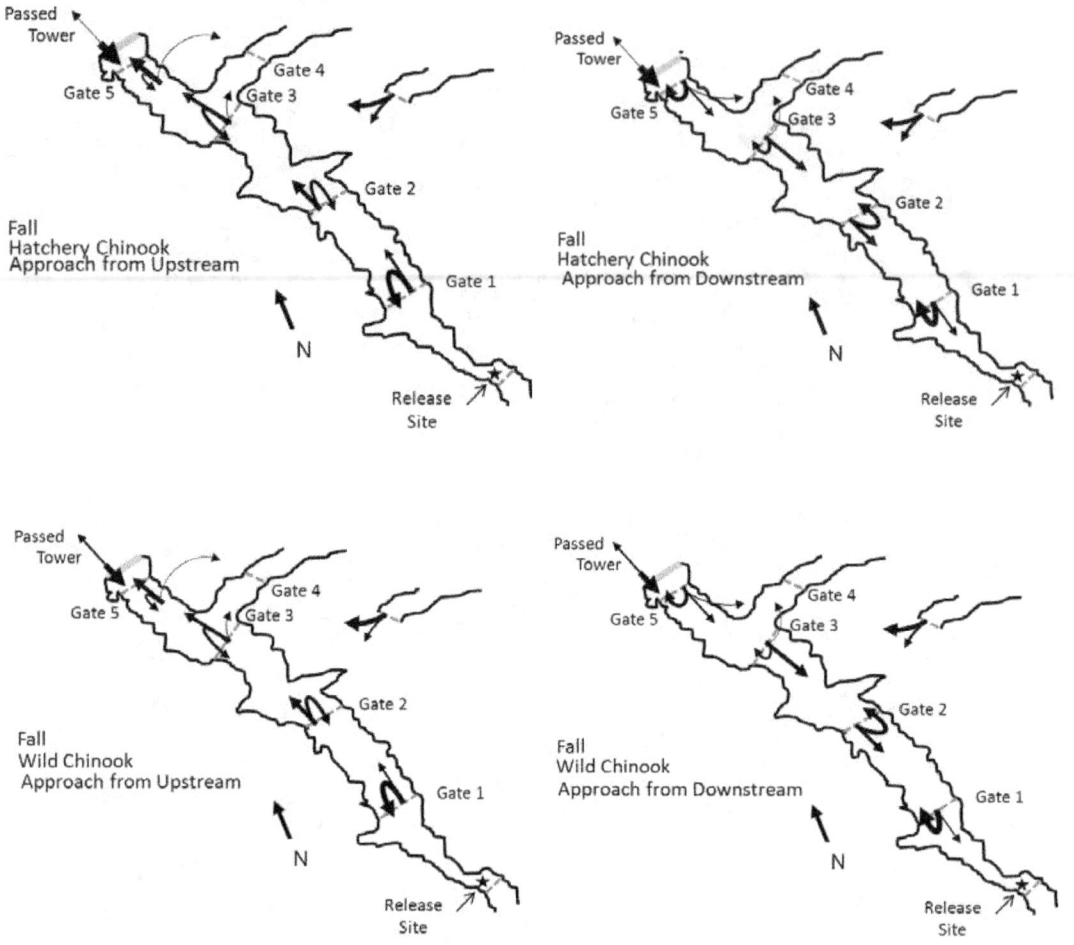

Figure 16. Transition probabilities of hatchery and wild fish released into Cougar Reservoir, Oregon, fall 2011. Relative width of arrows represents probabilities of moving from one array to an adjacent array based on the previous movement (see appendix table A1 for probabilities). Transition probabilities for gates 3 and 5 do not include fish coming from gate 4; transitions from gate 4 are shown to the right of each diagram.

Exceptions to the more prevalent upstream or downstream directional movements occurred when fish moved from the eastern arm of the reservoir (array 4) or from the log boom at the boat-restricted zone (array 5) after having been detected near the tower (array 7). Hatchery and wild fish moving from the eastern arm were about equally likely to move upstream or downstream during the spring period, whereas, during the fall period these fish were more likely to move upstream than downstream of the arm, irrespective of their previous location (appendix table A1). Fish near the log boom at the boat-restricted zone that had come from upstream generally were more likely to swim to the temperature control tower (spring, 0.72–0.75; fall 0.47–0.62), whereas fish at the log boom that had just come from the temperature control tower were about equally likely to swim back downstream to the tower as they were to continue swimming upstream. During the spring period, out of the 4,232 hatchery fish movements from array 5 to array 7, the probability of a fish passing the dam during one of these events was 0.01, whereas, out of 168 similar movements for wild fish, the probability of a fish passing the dam was 0.05. In the fall period, out of 3,337 hatchery fish movements from array 5 to the tower, the probability of a fish passing the dam was 0.03, whereas, out of the 476 similar movements for wild fish, the probability of a fish passing the dam was 0.24.

Effects of Dam Discharge on Downstream Fish Movements

An analysis of selected factors on the rates of downstream movement in two areas of the reservoir was conducted to determine if increasing dam discharge guided fish from upstream areas closer to the temperature control tower. The two areas were zone 3, a mid-reservoir area, and zone 5, the area from slightly upstream of the debris barrier to within about 100 m of the temperature control tower (to the system of hydrophones used to estimate fish positions; fig. 2). The analysis was stratified by approach direction as fish entered each zone (from upstream or downstream) based on results of transition probabilities indicating that fish movements through the reservoir were directed rather than random. The analysis was based on data combined from spring and fall periods. Data chosen for analysis included discharge ranges of 900–1,090 ft^3/s (low) and 1,500–1,690 ft^3/s (high), and elevation ranges of 1,540.0–1,570.0 ft (low) and 1,664.3–1,689.9 ft N (high), and data from 551 hatchery fish. Data from the 82 wild fish present during these conditions were omitted from the analysis owing the lack of data in some combinations of elevation and discharge groups.

An evaluation of the data and models indicated that downstream movement rates of hatchery fish from zones 3 and 5 were not higher at the high-discharge level than at the low-discharge level, and were not higher during low reservoir water elevation than during high elevation. There were several significant two-way interactions in the final model, which complicate interpretation of the model (table 7). The main effect of Diel (night relative to day) was not statistically significant, but was kept in the model because of its presence in significant interactions. The presence of significant interactions means the hazard ratios of the main factors reflect their effects only at the basal levels of the other main factors. For example, the hazard ratio of 1.805 for the Zone factor indicates that the downstream movement rate of fish from zone 5 (coded as zone = '1') was 1.805 times higher than the rate from zone 3 (coded as zone = '0'), but only during the day at low elevation and discharge levels. The interaction of Zone and Elevation (z_e) indicates that the effect of elevation on downstream movement rates is 2.272 times greater for zone 5 than for zone 3, and the lack of other interactions involving Zone indicates that the effects of Diel and Discharge were the same in each zone.

The predicted effects of elevation and discharge are mediated by diel period. The shortest predicted travel times through each zone were during high elevation and low discharge (fig. 17). The predicted travel times also are shorter through zone 5 than zone 3, a result that is likely affected by the difference in zone lengths and their proximities to the dam outlet. The results we present describe fish moving downstream as they entered the zones. The rates of downstream movement from each zone were lower for fish moving upstream when they entered the zones than for those moving downstream when they entered the zones.

The water temperature was warmer during the high-elevation level than during the low-elevation level. The water temperature (average of the three shallowest sensors on the string at the temperature control tower, the upper 13–19 ft) averaged 11.8°C (range 5.4–16.6°C) during the high-elevation level (spring and summer), and 5.5°C (range 4.5–6.7°C) during the low-elevation level (fall and winter).

Results from a computational-fluid-dynamics model by the COE indicate there were very low water velocities during the conditions examined in this analysis. The model predicts water velocities of about 0.02 ft/s (1.2 ft/min) or slower in most areas of the reservoir away from the temperature control tower (fig. 17). The model conditions in figure 18 are at a lower elevation (1,532 ft) than the conditions in the analysis (minimum 1,540.0 ft); therefore, the water velocities at the conditions examined are expected to be slightly lower than those in the figure.

Table 7. Regression coefficients from analysis of the effects of selected factors on the rates of downstream movement from reservoir zones 3 and 5 for juvenile Chinook salmon released into Cougar Reservoir, Oregon, spring and fall 2011.

[Pr > ChiSq = probability of a larger Chi-Square value under the hypothesis that the parameter estimate is zero, < is less than. Factors include zone (0 zone 3, 1 zone 5), elevation group (0 low, 1 high), diel period (diel, 0 day, 1 night), discharge (0 low, 1 high), and several two-way interactions (z_e, zone and elevation; e_p, elevation and diel period; e_d, elevation and discharge; p_d, diel period and discharge. Each row is based on one degree of freedom. The data were chosen to represent two elevation ranges (low 1,540.0–1,570.0 feet (ft), high 1,664.3–1,689.9 ft) and two discharge ranges (low 900–1,090 cubic feet per second (ft^3/s), high 1,500–1,690 ft^3/s). Hazard ratios and confidence intervals of variables involved in interactions represent the effect at the basal level of the other factor]

Variable	Parameter estimate	Standard error	Chi-Square	Pr > ChiSq	Hazard ratio	95-percent hazard ratio confidence limits	
Zone	0.5904	0.0879	45.12	<0.0001	1.805	1.519	2.144
Elevation	0.4878	0.1405	12.06	0.0005	1.629	1.237	2.145
Diel	-0.0801	0.1266	0.40	0.5269	0.923	0.72	1.183
Discharge	-0.5588	0.1292	18.71	<0.0001	0.572	0.444	0.737
z_e	0.8208	0.1237	44.03	<0.0001	2.272	1.783	2.896
e_p	-0.6606	0.1276	26.79	<0.0001	0.517	0.402	0.663
e_d	0.3004	0.1315	5.22	0.0224	1.350	1.044	1.747
p_d	0.7376	0.1294	32.49	<0.0001	2.091	1.623	2.695

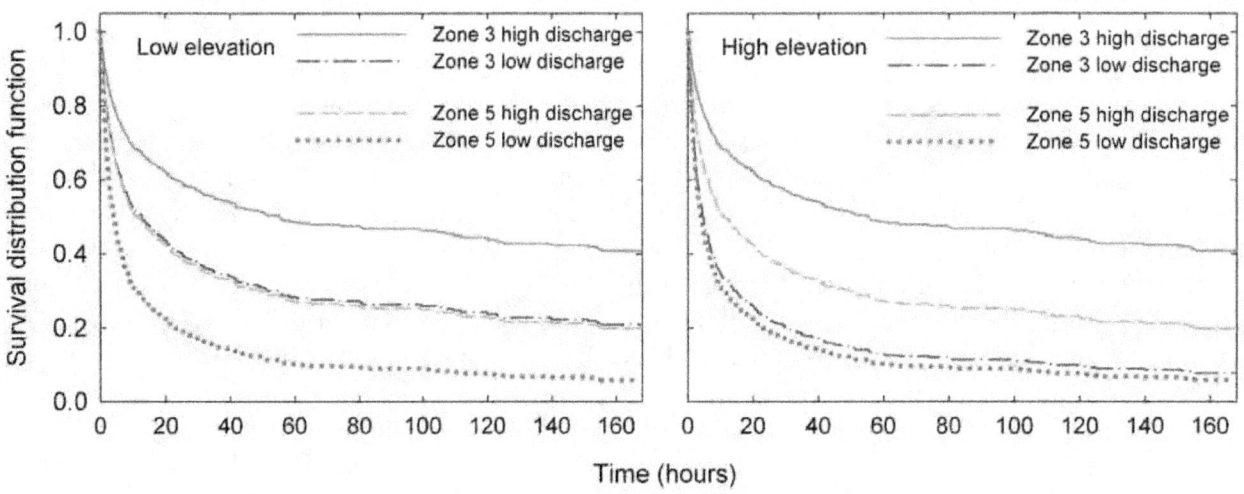

Figure 17. Graphs showing predicted travel times through zones 3 and 5 for juvenile Chinook salmon released into Cougar Reservoir, Oregon, spring and fall 2011. Predictions are at different elevations and discharges based on the regression coefficients in table 7.

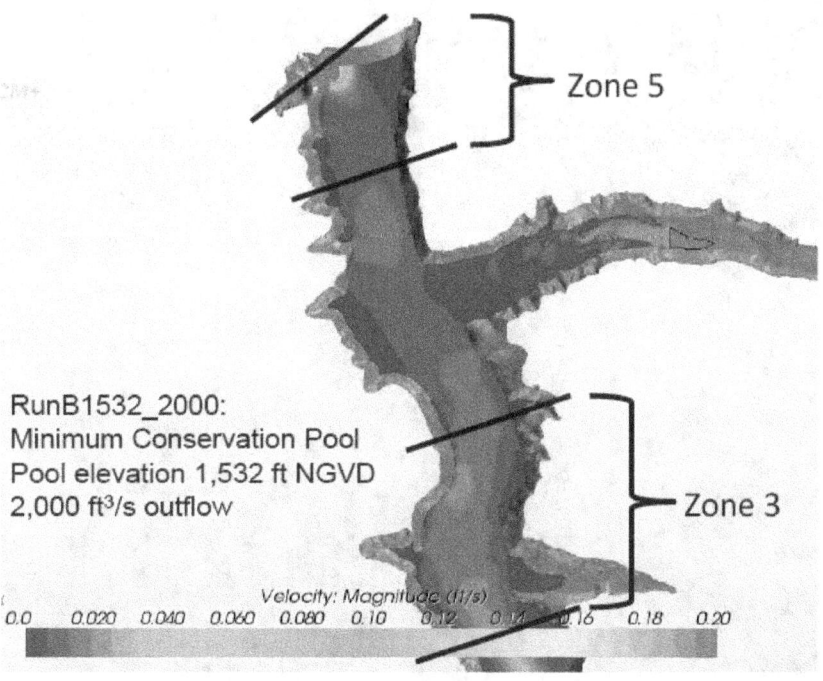

Figure 18. Surface-water velocities in feet per second (ft/s) predicted from a computational fluid dynamics model of Cougar Reservoir, Oregon. The conditions are an elevation of 1,532 feet National Geodetic Vertical Datum of 1929 and a dam discharge of 2,000 cubic feet per second (ft³/s) (provided by Liza Roy, U.S. Army Corps of Engineers, April 5, 2012).

Locations of Fish near the Temperature Control Tower

The system of hydrophones within about 100 m from the temperature control tower is designed to allow estimation of fish positions. A scatter plot of fish positions from these data is shown in figure 19. We summarized estimated fish positions at a specific dam operation to illustrate the location of tagged fish near the tower. Data from fish that eventually were within 10 m of the face of the temperature control tower are summarized in figure 20. The plots are of the positions of the fish during their first hour in the monitored area (where they approached from) and during their last 10 minutes prior to getting within 10 m of the tower (where they ended up). The data indicate that fish approached the tower from directly south (upstream) or slightly to the east of the tower. This pattern is apparent in plots of data from hatchery and wild fish, though there are fewer wild fish. The fish of both origins primarily were directly upstream of the tower entrance during their last 10 min in the detection area, indicating they were directly in front of the outlet rather than off to one side or another.

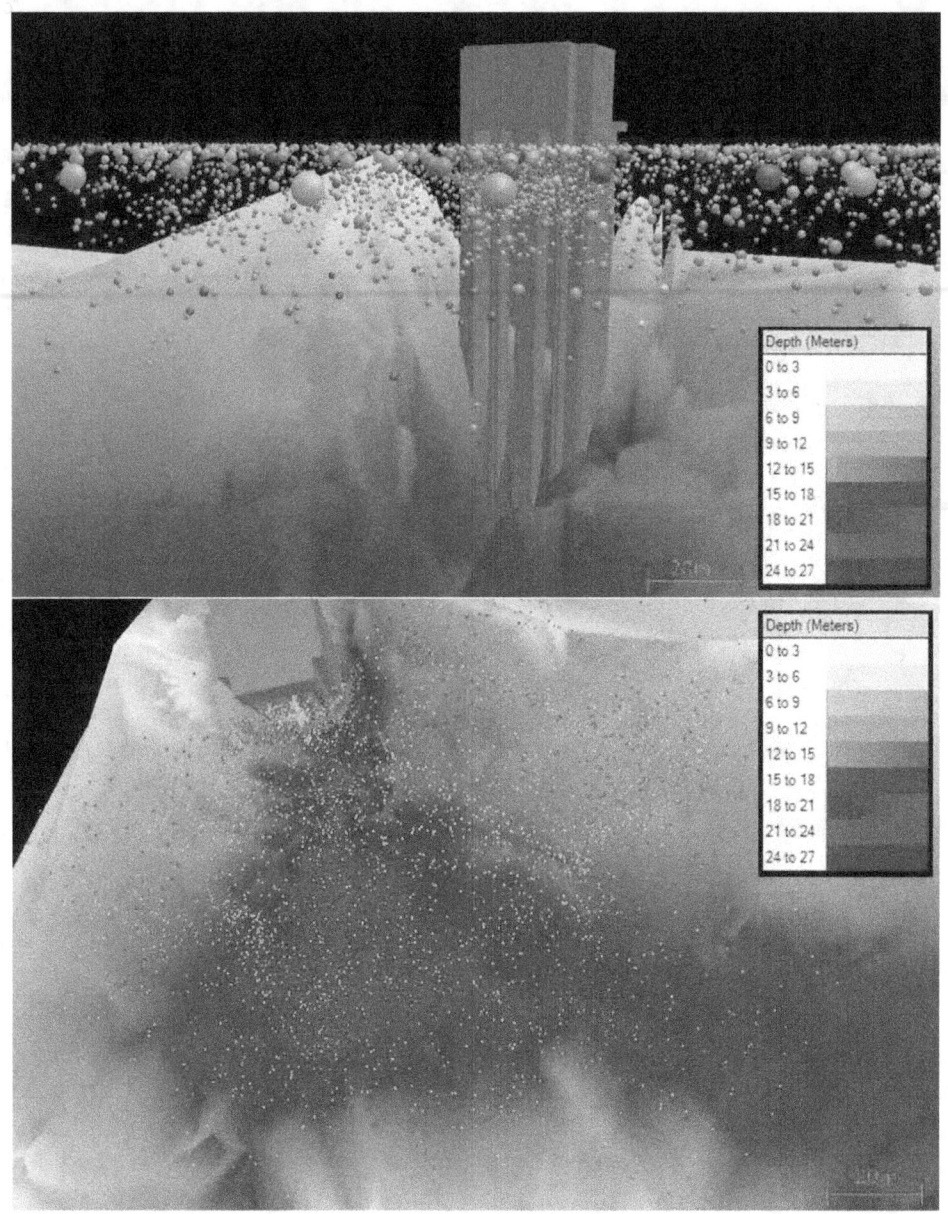

Figure 19. Three-dimensional fish position estimates near the temperature control tower for yearling Chinook salmon released into Cougar Reservoir, Oregon, spring 2011. The data shown are from the 24-hour period from June 29, 2011, at 6 a.m. to June 30, 2011, at 6 a.m. The top image is a cross-sectional view, and the bottom image is an aerial view. Symbol colors indicate individual fish, and their relative sizes as spheres in the top image represent distance from the viewer (larger is closer). Legend is for reservoir bathymetry.

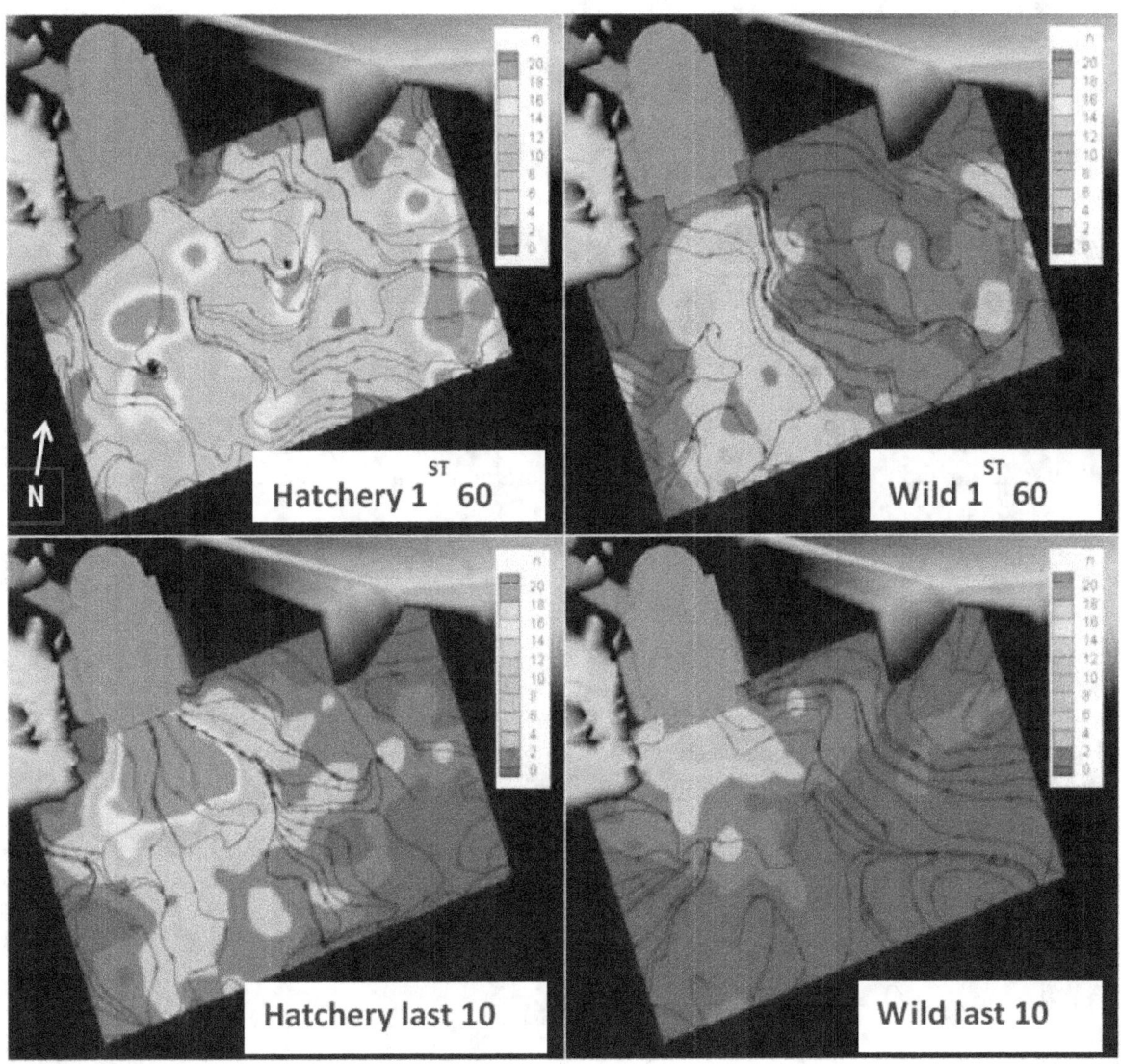

Figure 20. Flood plots and movement vectors of subyearling Chinook salmon released into Cougar Reservoir, Oregon, fall 2011. Plots are based on fish that were within approximately 100 meters of the temperature control tower in 2011 when the discharge was 1,000 cubic feet per second (ft^3/s) and the elevation was 1,600 feet National Geodetic Vertical Datum of 1929. The legend indicates values of the number of fish represented. The movement vectors represent the general movement directions of fish in the nearby area.

Dam Passage

The seasonal timing of tagged fish that passed the dam is indicated by vertical bars in figure 6. Dam passage occurred primarily during periods of elevated discharge, and was most pronounced during the fall period when reservoir elevations were low. Dates of dam passage ranged from March 26 to July 29, 2011 for fish released in the spring, and from October 18, 2011 to February 20, 2012 for fish released in the fall. There were two small peaks of dam passage during the spring between April 30 and June 5, 2011, followed by another peak on June 27, 2011. Most dam passage occurred from November 1 to December 10, 2011 and from January 5 to 29, 2012. This report includes data up to February 27, 2012. The spring period ended on July 24, 2012; however, one fish passed the dam on July 27, 2012.

Most presumed dam passage events occurred at night. Only 13 of the 166 passage events occurred during the day (fig. 21). We do not know the time of passage for two fish that passed the dam after their acoustic transmitters stopped working (both were detected at PIT systems downstream). One fish was detected at Willamette Falls Dam on July 11, 2011, at 7:37 a.m., and the second fish was collected in the Cougar RO tailrace screw trap operated by the Oregon Department of Fish and Wildlife (ODFW) on November 12, 2011, at 1:06 p.m.

A total of 48 hatchery fish and 6 wild fish are presumed to have passed the dam during the spring period. This includes the one wild fish that passed the dam after its acoustic tag stopped working and was detected by the PIT system at Willamette Falls Dam (last acoustic transmitter data was received 100 days after the fish's release). Five hatchery and 2 wild fish had passage events during the after the tag life cutoff (past the 90th percentile of expected tag life). Therefore, during the spring period, a total of 43 of 411 hatchery fish are presumed to have passed the dam (passage rate 10.5 percent), and a total of 4 of 26 wild fish are presumed to have passed the dam (passage rate 15.4 percent). A total of 36 of 43 hatchery fish (83.7 percent) and 4 of the 4 wild fish (100.0 percent) tagged in the spring had passage events during the night.

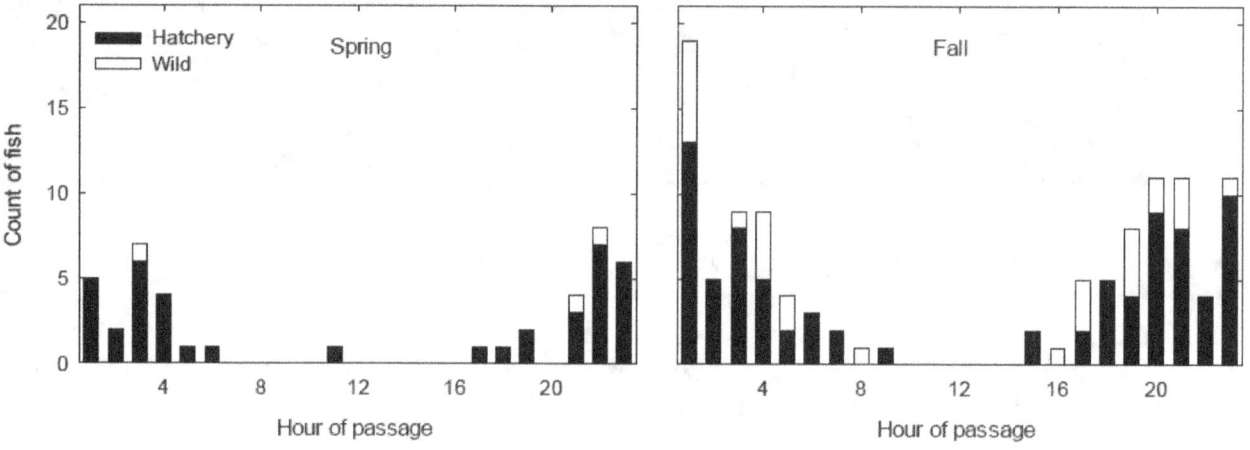

Figure 21. Graphs showing hour of known passage of juvenile Chinook salmon released into Cougar Reservoir, Oregon, for fish tagged during spring and fall 2011.

There were a total of 90 hatchery and 30 wild fish passage events during the fall period. This includes the one hatchery fish that passed after its acoustic tag stopped working and was detected by ODFW personnel at the RO screw trap in the Cougar Dam tailrace (last acoustic transmitter data was received 40 days after the fish's release). One hatchery fish and no wild fish passage events occurred after the tag life cutoff. Therefore, during the fall period, a total of 89 of the 356 hatchery fish had passage events (25.0 percent), and a total of 30 of 117 wild fish had passage events (16.9 percent). In the fall period a total of 85 of 89 hatchery fish passage events (95.5 percent) and 28 of 30 wild fish passage events (93.3 percent) were at night.

Reservoir and Dam Passage Efficiencies

Season-wide estimates of reservoir passage efficiency (RPE) were higher than estimates of dam passage efficiency (DPE). Estimates of reservoir passage efficiency (RPE) ranged from 0.692 to 0.864 and were similar for hatchery and wild fish (table 8). Estimates of DPE of wild fish were numerically greater than those from hatchery fish, but the small number of tagged wild fish resulted in confidence intervals overlapping those of the hatchery fish. The estimated DPE of hatchery fish tagged in the spring period (0.135) was lower than that of hatchery fish in the fall period (0.296), but DPE of wild fish was similar in both groups of fish (0.333 spring period, 0.330 fall period). Few wild fish were available for the estimate, so the confidence intervals for wild fish DPE are large.

The DPE generally was similar between spring and fall periods when grouped by reservoir elevation. The spring period only includes the highest reservoir elevation grouping (1,571-1,690 ft NVGD 29), and their DPE was similar to that of the fall period in that elevation range (table 9).

Table 8. Season-wide estimates of passage efficiencies of juvenile Chinook salmon released into Cougar Reservoir, Oregon, spring and fall 2011.

[Reservoir Passage efficiency (RPE) is the proportion of fish released near the head of the reservoir detected near the boat-restricted zone line, and dam passage efficiency (DPE) is the proportion of the fish detected at the boat-restricted zone line that passed the dam. Sample size is the number of tagged fish in the denominator of the estimate]

Period	Origin	Metric	Sample size	Estimate	Standard error	95-percent confidence interval	
						Lower	Upper
Spring	Hatchery	RPE	411	0.864	0.017	0.831	0.897
		DPE	355	0.135	0.018	0.100	0.171
	Wild	RPE	26	0.692	0.091	0.515	0.870
		DPE	18	0.333	0.111	0.116	0.551
Fall	Hatchery	RPE	356	0.854	0.019	0.817	0.891
		DPE	304	0.296	0.026	0.245	0.347
	Wild	RPE	117	0.778	0.038	0.702	0.853
		DPE	91	0.330	0.049	0.233	0.426

Table 9. Reservoir-elevation based estimates of dam passage efficiency of juvenile Chinook salmon released into Cougar Reservoir, Oregon, spring and fall 2011.

[Dam passage efficiency (DPE) is the proportion of the fish detected at the boat-restricted zone line that passed the dam. Sample size is the number of tagged fish in the denominator of the estimate. < is less than]

Period	Origin	Elevation range (feet)	Sample size	Estimate	Standard error	95-percent confidence interval	
						Lower	Upper
Spring	Hatchery	1,690–1,571	355	0.135	0.018	0.100	0.171
	Wild	1,690–1,571	18	0.333	0.111	0.116	0.551
Fall	Hatchery	1,690–1,571	278	0.209	0.024	0.161	0.256
		<1,571–1,532	196	0.163	0.026	0.112	0.215
		<1,532–1,516	43	0.000	0.000	0.000	0.000
	Wild	1,690–1,571	77	0.299	0.052	0.197	0.401
		<1,571–1,532	69	0.101	0.036	0.030	0.173
		<1,532–1,516	15	0.000	0.000	0.000	0.000

Data from the fall period are available from the entire range of elevations from full conservation pool to less than the minimum conservation pool (1,532 ft), enabling estimates of DPE across the full range of elevations. The estimates of DPE were proportional to reservoir elevation (table 9). This is likely owing to the pattern of reservoir elevation changes across time, resulting in the presence of the highest elevation range during the normal fall drawdown period, beginning in September 2011, as well as during a wet period in January 2012. Most dam passage occurred during short periods in November 2011 and in January 2012. No tagged fish passed the dam when the elevation was below 1,532 ft.

Effects of Selected Variables on Dam Passage Rates

Using an approach similar to that used for the analysis of downstream movements within the reservoir, data from two discharge levels and two elevations were chosen to evaluate the potential effects of several variables on dam passage rates. The data used in this analysis were a combination of those from the spring and fall periods. Recall from the section, "Methods," that the data chosen for this analysis included discharge ranges of 800–1,190 ft^3/s (low) and 1,410–1,800 ft^3/s (high), elevation ranges of 1,545.0–1,583.9 ft (low) and 1,670.0–1,689.8 ft (high), and data from 365 to 488 hatchery fish and 60 to 79 wild fish, depending on the area. The analysis was based on fish within several distances (areas) from the temperature control tower, based on estimates of three-dimensional positions. The groups of data were for fish within 75, 55, and 35 m from the tower. Data from areas nearer than 35 m from the tower were too sparse for this analysis.

The variables remaining in the final models generally were similar. Final models from the two largest areas included elevation, diel period, and discharge (table 10). Diel period was not included as a potential factor in the analysis using data from the area within 35 m from the tower because of sparse data (no passage events during the day in some combinations of other factors), but the resulting final model otherwise was similar to the previous models. The models indicated that dam passage rate was greatest during low elevation, at night, and during high discharge.

Table 10. Regression coefficients from analysis of the effects of selected factors on the rate of dam passage of juvenile Chinook salmon released into Cougar Reservoir, Oregon, spring and fall 2011, that were estimated to be within 75 meters of the face of the temperature control tower.

[Results are based on distances of fish from the temperature control tower estimated from three dimensional positions. Pr > ChiSq = probability of a larger Chi-Square value under the hypotheses that the parameter estimate is zero, < is less than. Factors included origin (0 hatchery, 1 wild), elevation group (0 low, 1 high), diel period (diel, 0 day, 1 night), discharge (0 low, 1 high), and all possible two-way interactions. Each row is based on one degree of freedom. The data were chosen to represent two elevation ranges (low 1545.0–1583.90 feet, high 1670.0–1689.8 feet) and two discharge ranges (low 800–1,190 cubic feet per second [ft^3/s], high 1,410–1,800 ft^3/s). Results from variables with a Pr > Chisq $\leq$ 0.05 are shown.]

Distance to tower	Variable	Parameter estimate	Standard error	Chi-Square	Pr > ChiSq	Hazard ratio	95-percent hazard ratio confidence limits	
< 75 m	Elevation	-0.6654	0.2769	5.78	0.0162	0.514	0.299	0.884
	Diel	2.1833	0.3540	38.04	<.0001	8.876	4.435	17.763
	Discharge	1.3087	0.2261	33.51	<.0001	3.701	2.377	5.765
< 55 m	Elevation	-0.7537	0.2912	6.70	0.0096	0.471	0.266	0.833
	Diel	2.2243	0.3754	35.11	<.0001	9.247	4.431	19.299
	Discharge	1.3677	0.2366	33.41	<.0001	3.926	2.469	6.243
< 35 m[1]	Elevation	-0.9345	0.3419	7.47	0.0063	0.393	0.2010	0.7680
	Discharge	1.2984	0.2767	22.02	<.0001	3.664	2.1300	6.3010

[1] Diel not included in models because of sparse data

Fish origin was not a significant factor in any of the models, and data from hatchery and wild fish were subsequently pooled. The lack of a significant origin effect indicates that the passage rates of wild fish were not different than those of hatchery fish; however, the data were primarily from hatchery fish. The lack of significant interactions between origin and the other factors indicates that the effects of the remaining significant factors were similar for hatchery and wild fish based on the data and models.

The coefficients for elevation, diel period, and discharge were similar among models. The results indicate that dam passage rate at the high elevation was 39.3–51.4 percent of that at the low elevation (table 10; hazard ratio range 0.393–0.514 equates to 39.3–51.4 percent of the low elevation rate). The estimated hazard ratios for elevation decrease slightly as distance to the dam decreases, but their 95-percent confidence intervals overlap considerably, suggesting the differences are trivial. Dam passage rate was about 9 times greater during the night than during the day (hazard ratios of 8.876 and 9.247). Dam passage rate was nearly four times greater at the high discharge level than at the low discharge level (hazard ratio range 3.664–3.701). The lack of significant two-way interactions between elevation, diel period, or discharge indicates that their effects were not interdependent.

The relative effects of elevation, diel period and discharge on dam passage rates can be seen in predictions of the time needed to pass the dam. As an example, figure 22 shows predictions of the time needed to pass the dam based on the regression equations in table 10 for fish within 75 m from the tower. Differences between the two plots show the predicted effect of elevation on dam passage times. Under the best-case scenario for passage rates (high discharge at night), predicted dam passage within 12 hours is 7.8 percent of the population within 75 m of the tower at high elevation and 14.5 percent at the low elevation. Under the worst-case scenario (low discharge and high elevation during the day), predicted dam passage within 12 hours of fish within 75 m of the tower is small: less than 1 percent of tagged fish."

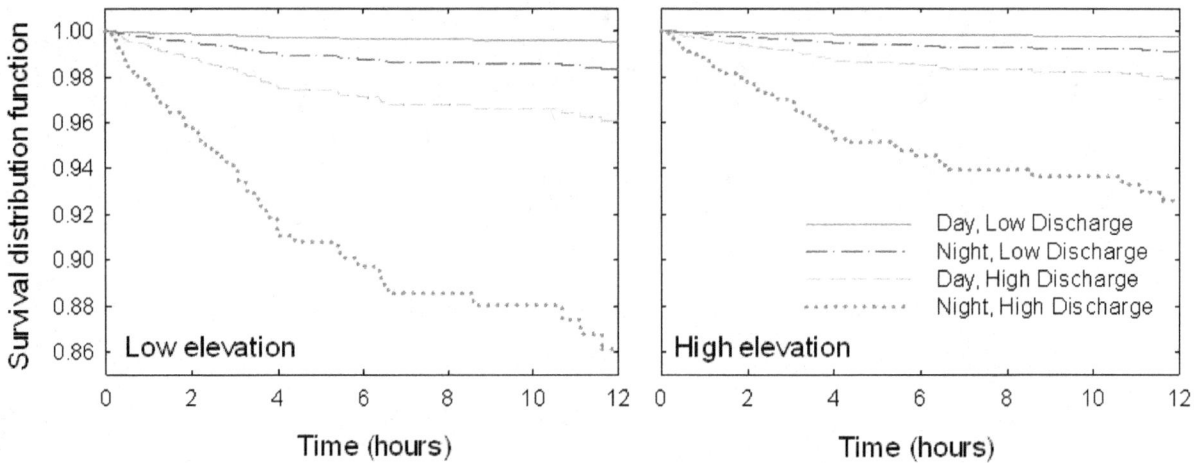

Figure 22. Graphs showing predicted time for juvenile Chinook salmon within 75 meters of the temperature control tower to pass Cougar Dam, Oregon, during various conditions of forebay elevation, diel period, and dam discharge based on regression coefficients in table 10.

The water temperatures were slightly warmer during the high-elevation level than during the low-elevation level. The water temperatures (average of the three shallowest sensors on the string at the temperature control tower, the upper 13–19 ft) during the conditions used in the analysis and summarized in table 8 averaged 9.4 °C (range 5.4–13.4 °C) during the high-elevation level (spring and summer), and 5.6 °C (range 4.4–7.1 °C) during the low-elevation level (fall and winter).

Discussion

This report summarizes information collected from juvenile Chinook salmon implanted with acoustic transmitters released into Cougar Reservoir during the spring and fall 2011. The purpose of the study is to provide information to aid in making decisions about potential future data needs or operations to consider in developing downstream fish passage solutions for juvenile salmonids.

We based our inferences on fish from a local hatchery as well as wild fish captured from within Cougar Reservoir. Wild fish were difficult to capture, and represent a small percentage of the total tagged fish. This was particularly evident in spring, when the average catch rate was 1 fish per 7 hauls of a Lampara seine and wild fish constituted 28 of the 443 fish tagged. The catch rates of wild fish in the Lampara seine were much higher in the fall than in the spring, at least partially because of the schooling behavior that was noted only in the fall, resulting in wild fish representing 118 of 476 tagged fish. Because the fish of interest are the wild fish within the reservoir, comparisons of hatchery and wild fish were included in analyses where sample sizes of wild fish were sufficient.

The tagged fish in Cougar Reservoir moved throughout the reservoir and did not appear to be concentrated in one zone more than another. Their movements within the reservoir were directed, rather than random, and fish often made repeated trips between the upstream and downstream boundaries of the reservoir. The time of detections, an indication of the timing of fish movements, was primarily at night during the fall period, but generally there was no discernible pattern in the time of detections of fish during the spring period. This also was true for the timing of fish detections near the temperature control tower, which were most prevalent near dawn during the fall period. Most fish reached the zone within about 100 m from the temperature control tower at least once, and many fish entered the zone dozens of times. This behavior likely increases the probability of dam passage by providing multiple opportunities to be near the dam outlet and at risk of dam passage.

Dam passage rates were related to diel period, dam discharge, and reservoir elevation. Diel period was by far the most influential factor in our analysis, but this result could differ based on the levels of the other variables examined. More than 89 percent of the dam passage of tagged fish occurred at night. The rate of dam passage at night of fish as far away as 75 m from the tower was about 9 times the rate during the day. Dam passage rates were nearly four times greater at a discharge of 1,410–1,800 ft^3/s compared to a discharge of 800–1,190 ft^3/s. Dam passage when the reservoir elevation was 1,545–1,584 ft was about twice the rate when the elevation was 1,670–1,960 ft. This finding is consistent with presence of higher water velocity at a given discharge when the reservoir occupies a smaller volume. The results indicate that the conditions most beneficial for increasing dam passage rates are high discharge and low elevation during the night.

Dam passage occurred often during the spring period, but in low numbers compared to the fall period. Most dam passage occurred during short periods in November, December, and January during conditions of high discharge and varied reservoir elevation. Fish passage may have been more concentrated during the fall period than in the spring period because passage rate (passage of available fish per hour) is much greater at night than in the day, and the nights are longest in the fall and winter. This results in conditions conducive to the presence of a higher dam passage rate for a longer period than during the spring and summer. Dam passage may have been more widespread but occurred at a lower rate during the spring period because the conditions conducive to higher passage rates were less prevalent. There was no dam passage detected between July 28 and October 19, but there were few tagged fish with active transmitters in the reservoir during that period. Daily catches of juvenile salmonids in rotary screw traps downstream from the dam during that period were among the lowest of the year, suggesting the absence of tagged fish did not appreciably bias our seasonal estimates of dam passage (Romer and others, 2012).

The estimated DPE was proportional to reservoir elevation, which seems contrary to the generally observed condition of highest passage during winter. Analyses of dam passage rates from this study indicate passage rates are greatest during low elevation, which is a condition commonly associated with winter operations. This is consistent with catches of fish in rotary screw traps in the dam tailraces (Romer and others, 2012), and trap catches in the McKenzie River prior to construction of the temperature control tower (Zakel and Reed, 1984). The proportional relation between DPE and reservoir elevation from our study is owing to the patterns of fish passage and reservoir elevations during fall and winter of 2011–12. Most dam passage of our tagged fish occurred in November 2011 and January 2012 when the elevation range was 1,571–1,690 ft. The remaining passage events during this time occurred in November and December 2011 when elevation range was 1,532–1,570 ft. The dam passage events in

January 2012 coincided with a peak in precipitation and reservoir elevation and, therefore, represented passage during the 1,571–1,690 ft elevation range usually associated with the beginning of reservoir drawdown rather than conditions in January. In this case is appears that the effects of high discharge on passage rates were more influential than those of reservoir elevation.

The observational nature of the study constrains the types of analyses that can be performed because the variables of interest often occur at different levels infrequently (for example, discharge) or are correlated with one another (for example, water temperature and reservoir elevation). Much has been learned about the behavior of juvenile Chinook salmon in the reservoir since the beginning of this study that may enable future evaluations of the effects of various dam operations or structures in a more controlled manner. For example, prior to this study, little was known about where the fish resided in the reservoir, with what probability they would reach the temperature control tower, that there was a diel difference in dam passage rates, and how various factors affected dam passage rates.

The process of fish passage at barriers may be considered a series of processes beginning with fish movement toward the barrier and ending with passage through it. Using such a framework allows the process ending in successful passage to be divided into components that can be separately evaluated to facilitate design and to diagnose problems. Castro-Santos and Haro (2010) divided the process into "guidance," getting near enough to the desired entrance to detect its presence; "attraction", entering the desired route conditional on guidance to it; and "passage", passing through the desired route conditional on attraction into it. A model with more facets was suggested by Sweeny and others (2007) in which they identified "approach", "discovery", decision", "conveyance", and outfall". Here we will use the simpler terms of Castro-Santos and Haro (2010), although the concepts are similar.

In Cougar Reservoir, guidance is present, but the evidence we examined does not support guidance of fish far upstream of the temperature control tower being affected by typical dam operations. The fact that most fish make repeated trips throughout the reservoir and get near the temperature control tower many times may be used as evidence of guidance based on what appears to be a common behavior. The rate of downstream movement of fish from zones 3 and 5 was not greater during the higher of the two discharge levels we examined, indicating that guidance from those zones towards the dam outlet was not enhanced by those dam operations. The rate of downstream movement was actually highest during the low discharge level examined. This result likely is owing to the very low water velocities present in these reservoir zones at the discharge levels used in the analysis. Predictions from a computational-fluid-dynamics model suggest this is the case.

Attraction to the outlet is obviously present at some level, but we could not make a quantitative estimate from the fish tagged in 2011. The acoustic telemetry system at Cougar Dam during this study was not suitable to track fish into and out of the temperature control tower, because all the hydrophones were outside the structure. However, Khan and others (2012), in a year-long study of fish movements based on acoustic imaging, found that fish in the size range of juvenile salmonids were present near the entrance to the temperature control tower nearly continuously throughout the year, indicating attraction was present much of the time. A hydrophone was added inside the tower during spring 2012 to enable estimates of attraction in subsequent studies.

Poor entrainment appears to be one factor limiting passage at Cougar Dam, but it may not be the greatest factor. Once again, the work of Khan and others (2012) indicates fish can swim into and out of the temperature control tower, and we have visually observed this behavior in shallow fish from within the tower. Khan and others (2012) found that increases in the net movements of fish into the tower were greatest during spring and late fall and winter, coinciding with periods of peak fish passage. Data we collected from acoustic-tagged fish in 2012 indicates fish rarely leave the tower after they enter it, and that attraction (that is, getting inside the tower) may be the greater limiting factor.

In many cases, the results from wild and hatchery fish were similar, or the results suggested hatchery fish would be reasonable surrogates for wild fish for studies of their movements and dam passage. Movement probabilities within the reservoir generally were similar between hatchery and wild fish. Movements of both groups were directional in most comparisons, meaning that fish that were moving upstream tended to continue upstream and those moving downstream tended to continue downstream until passing the dam or turning around. The probability of reaching the area near the temperature control tower at least once was similar between hatchery and wild fish. In data from fish released in the spring, which included few wild fish, the evidence was equivocal about a difference in probability of reaching the tower between fish of different origins. In data from fish released in the fall, when there were more than 100 wild fish released, there was moderate support against a difference in this probability between fish of different origins. The time of day wild fish were detected moving within the reservoir was more variable than hatchery fish during the spring period and neither group showed a discernible diel pattern at most sites. In the fall period, fish from both groups were detected more frequently during the night than during the day. Fish origin was not a significant contributor to models of dam passage rates and the effects of diel period, discharge, and elevation on dam passage rates were similar between origins when there were sufficient data for comparisons. The estimated DPE of wild fish was slightly greater than that of hatchery fish, but the error about the estimate was large because of the small number of tagged wild fish available. The results of this study suggest that conditions that favor passage of hatchery fish also will favor passage of wild fish.

All wild fish examined were hosts to parasitic copepods, whereas only one of the hatchery fish examined prior to release had copepods. Pre-release mortality of wild fish was much higher than that of hatchery fish, presumably related to the load of parasitic copepods reducing the ability of wild fish to cope with the stressors associated with capture, tagging, and handling. This may represent an important difference between the origins if the wild fish are less able than hatchery fish to cope with the potential stressors of operations or structures implemented for downstream fish passage. Interestingly, one tagged hatchery fish released without parasitic copepods was observed with them when recovered by ODFW in a rotary screw trap in the tailrace of Cougar Dam on November 18, 2011, 71 days after release.

Downstream fish passage can be increased by manipulating dam operations based on the results from this study. However, the rate of dam passage of fish near the temperature control tower was low relative to fish passage rates at certain other hydroelectric dams. Models indicate that at Cougar Dam even under moderately advantageous levels of discharge (1,410–1,800 ft^3/s) and reservoir elevation (1,545–1,584 ft NVGD 29) predicted dam passage of fish within 12 hours is only 14.5 percent of the fish within 75 m from the tower. For comparison, at Little Goose Dam on the Snake River in Washington State, the dam passage of radio-tagged yearling Chinook salmon was estimated at more than 10 percent of the forebay population every hour (Beeman and others, 2010; the Little Goose Dam forebay in that study was defined as about 0.75 km × 1.5 km in size). Little Goose Dam impounds a run-of-river reservoir with little storage capacity, meaning nearly all water arriving from upstream is passed downstream shortly thereafter. Upper Baker Dam in northern Washington State has a recently installed fish collector that appears to be effective in collecting juvenile salmonids. Upper Baker Dam is more similar to Cougar Dam than Little Goose Dam. The fish collector at Upper Baker Dam reportedly collected about 75 percent of the tagged (freeze branded) juvenile coho salmon (*Oncorhynchus kisutch*) and about 60 percent of the tagged juvenile sockeye salmon (*Oncorhynchus nerka*) released upstream between February 24 and August 3, 2010 (Puget Sound Energy, 2012). The total number of fish collected in this $50-million system at Upper Baker Dam in 2010 was 517,592. The Baker Gulper was designed to guide fish into gradually increasing water velocities over an inclined plane of approach, leading to a water velocity high enough to entrain fish, similar to the attributes Haro and others (1998) and Sweeney and others (2007) found to be common in other successful surface flow outlets.

The vertical gradient in water temperature present in Cougar Reservoir during part of the year complicates accurate estimation of three-dimensional positions of fish. Position estimates are affected by the speed of sound in water, which varies with water temperature. The positioning algorithm we used for the analyses in this report was based on a static water temperature. As such, the fish positions estimated during periods of vertical water temperature gradients, particularly the summer and early fall periods, are less accurate than those during periods with less temperature variation. A temperature-gradient modification to the current algorithm was nearly complete at the time of this report (2013).

We recommend that data from this and future studies of fish approach and passage at Willamette Basin dams be analyzed and reported in a standard manner to enable identification of causal mechanisms affecting guidance, attraction, and passage, and to facilitate comparisons among studies. Studies of fish passage at dams on tributaries of the Willamette River are increasing in number and location; identifying common analytical methods and reporting metrics will simplify comparisons among studies and foster efficient learning. We suggest that time-to-event methods be used to describe rates of dam passage and other pertinent events when suitable data are available. These methods make efficient use of the data from all subjects at risk of an event such as dam passage (rather than focusing only on subjects that experience the event), enable the use of time-varying covariates, and perform efficiently with skewed data that are common in studies of fish migration (Hosmer and Lemeshow, 1999; Castro-Santos and Haro, 2003; Castro-Santos and Perry, 2012). We also recommend that standard distances from passage routes or structures be used to evaluate guidance, approach, and passage (metrics described by Castro-Santos and Haro, 2010), as well as other metrics such as discovery efficiency and entrance efficiency (as recommend by Sweeney and others, 2007). Because physical environments differ among dams, a single distance need not be used, but a series of standard distances could be adopted. The distances from the dam outlet we used in analyses of dam passage were chosen arbitrarily to illustrate the changing effects of diel period, discharge, and elevation with distance from the outlet. There may be more meaningful distances in terms of providing information useful to the design of alternative operations or structures to enhance downstream fish passage.

Acknowledgments

Many people assisted with this study. The State of Oregon staff at the McKenzie River Fish Hatchery provided study fish and holding space, and were gracious in allowing us to use their facility. The staff at Cougar Dam assisted us in many aspects of logistics at the site. Fred Monzyk and his staff of the Oregon Department of Fish and Wildlife provided wild fish from their Oneida Lake trap. Noah Adams, Theresa "Marty" Liedtke, Matt Sholtis, Dana Shurtleff, and Nick Swyers of the U.S. Geological Survey assisted with field work and data analysis. Dave Griffith, Scott Fielding, Rich Piaskowski, Chad Helms, and Liza Roy of the U.S. Army Corps of Engineers, Portland District, arranged contracts and provided helpful information and coordination for the study. Funding for this project was provided by the U.S. Army Corps of Engineers, Portland District, Contract W66QKZ03023085.

References Cited

Allison, P.D., 1995, Survival analysis using SAS®—A practical guide: Cary, North Carolina, SAS Institute Inc., 292 p.

Beeman, J.W., Braatz, A.C., Hansel, H.C., Fielding, S.D., Haner, P.V., Hansen, G.S., Shurtleff, D.J., Sprando, J.M., and Rondorf, D.W., 2010, Approach, passage, and survival of juvenile salmonids at Little Goose Dam, Washington—Post-construction evaluation of a temporary spillway weir, 2009: U.S. Geological Survey Open-File Report 2010-1224, 101 p. (Also available at *http://pubs.usgs.gov/of/2010/1224/*.)

Beeman, J.W., Hansel, H.C., Hansen, A.C., Haner, P.V., Sprando, J.M., Smith, C.D., and Evans, S.D., 2012, Interim results from a study of the behavior of juvenile Chinook salmon at Cougar Reservoir and Dam, Oregon: U.S. Geological Survey Open-File Report 2012-1106.

Bhat, U.N., and Miller, G.K., 2002, Elements of applied stochastic processes: Hoboken, New Jersey, Wiley, 461 p.

Burnham, K.P., and Anderson, D.R., 2002, Model selection and multimodel inference—A practical information-theoretic approach: New York, Springer-Verlag, 488 p.

Castro-Santos, T., and Haro, A., 2003, Quantifying migratory delay—A new application of survival analysis methods: Canadian Journal of Fisheries and Aquatic Sciences, v. 60, p. 986–996.

Castro-Santos, T., and Haro, A., 2010, Fish guidance and passage at barriers, *in* Domenici, P., and Kapoor, B.G., eds., Fish locomotion—An eco-ethological perspective: Enfield, New Hampshire, Science Publishers, p. 62–89.

Castro-Santos, T., and Perry, R., 2012, Time-to-event analysis as a framework for quantifying fish passage performance, *in* Adams, N.S., Beeman, J.W., and Eiler, J.H., eds., Telemetry techniques—A user's guide for fisheries research: Bethesda, Maryland, American Fisheries Society, p. 427–452.

Cormack, R.M., 1964, Estimates of survival from the sighting of marked animals: Biometrika, v.51, no. 3–4, p. 429–438.

Deng, D.D., Weiland, M.A., Fu, T., Seim, T., LaMarche, B.L., Choi, E.Y., Carlson, T.J., and Eppard, B.M., 2011, A cabled acoustic telemetry system for detecting and tracking juvenile salmon—Part 2—Three-dimensional tracking and passage outcomes: Sensors, v. 11, p. 5561–5676.

Haro, A., Odeh, M., Noreika, J., and Castro-Santos, T., 1998, Effect of water acceleration on downstream migratory behavior of Atlantic salmon smolts and juvenile American shad at surface bypasses: Transactions of the American Fisheries Society, v. 127, p. 118–127.

Hosmer, D.W., and Lemeshow, S., 1999, Applied survival analysis—Regression modeling of time to event data: New York, Wiley, 386 p.

Johnson, G.E., Hedgepeth, J.B., Skalski, J.R., and Giorgi, A.E., 2004, A Markov chain analysis of fish movements to determine entrainment zones: Fisheries Research, v. 69, p. 349–358.

Jolly, G.M., 1965, Explicit estimates from capture-recapture data with both death and immigration-stochastic model: Biometrika, v. 52, no. 1–2, p. 225–247.

Khan F., Johnson, G.E., Royer, I.M., Phillips, N.R, Hughes, J.S., Fischer, E.S., and Ploskey, G.R., 2012, Acoustic imaging evaluation of juvenile salmonid behavior in the immediate forebay of the water temperature control tower at Cougar Dam, 2010: Pacific Northwest National Laboratory report PNNL-20625, 50 p.

McMichael, G.A., Eppard, M.B., Carlson, T.J., Carter, J.A., Ebberts, B.D., Brown, R.S., Weiland, M., Ploskey, G.R., Harnish, R.A., and Deng, Z.D., 2010, The juvenile salmon acoustic telemetry system—A new tool: Fisheries, v.35, no. 1, p. 9–22.

National Oceanic and Atmospheric Administration, 2008, Endangered Species Act section 7(a)(2) consultation biological opinion and Magnuson-Stevens Fishery Conservation and Management Act essential fish habitat consultation—Consultation on the Willamette River Basin Flood Control Project: National Oceanic and Atmospheric Administration Fisheries Log Number FINWRl2000/02117, June 11, 2008, accessed [March 25, 2013] at http://www.nwr.noaa.gov/hydropower/willamette_opinion/index.html.

Puget Sound Energy, 2012, Settlement agreement article 105 downstream fish passage implementation plan 2010 annual report: Puget Sound Energy report BAK.2012.0131.0549.PSE.BRCC, 34 p.

Romer, J.D., Monzyk, F.R., Emig, R., and Friesen, T.A., 2012, Juvenile salmonid outmigration monitoring at Willamette Valley Project reservoirs: Report of Oregon Department of Fish and Wildlife, Corvallis, Oregon to U.S. Army Corps of Engineers, contract W9127N-10-2-0008 Task order 6, Portland, Oregon, 47 p.

Seber, G.A.F., 1965, A note on the multiple-recapture census: Biometrika, v. 52, no. 1–2, p. 249–259.

Seber, G.A.F., 1982, The estimation of animal abundance and related parameters: New York, Macmillan, 654 p.

Surgical Protocols Steering Committee, 2011, Surgical protocols for implanting JSATS transmitters into juvenile salmonids for studies conducted for the U.S. Army Corps of Engineers: Report prepared by Surgical Protocols Steering Committee for U.S. Army Corps of Engineers, Portland, Oregon.

Sweeney, C.E., Giorgi, A.E., Johnson, G.E., Hall, R., and Miller, M., 2007, Surface bypass program comprehensive review report: ENSR Corporation document number 09000-399-0409, 494 p.

Titzler, P.S., McMichael, G.A., and Carter, J.A., 2010, Autonomous acoustic receiver deployment and mooring techniques for use in large rivers and estuaries: North American Journal of Fisheries Management, v. 30, p. 853–859.

Weiland, M.A., Deng, Z., Seim, T.A., LaMarche, B.L., Choi, E.Y., Fu, T., Carlson, T.J., Thronas, A.I., and Eppard, B.M., 2011, A cabled acoustic telemetry system for detecting and tracking juvenile salmon—Part 1—Engineering design and instrumentation: Sensors, v. 11, p. 5645–5660.

Weiland, M.A, Ploskey, G.R., Hughes, J.S., Deng, Z., Fu, T., Monter, T.J., Johnson, G.E., Khan, F., Wilberding, M.C., Cushing, A.W., Zimmerman, S.A., Faber, D.M., Durham, R.E., Townsend, R.L., Skalski, J.R., Kim, J., Fischer, E.S., and Meyer, M.M., 2009, Acoustic telemetry evaluation of juvenile salmonid passage and survival at John Day Dam with emphasis on the prototype surface flow outlet, 2008: Report PNNL-18890, Pacific Northwest National Laboratory, Richland, Washington, 259 p.

White, G.C., and Burnham, K.P., 1999, Program MARK—Survival estimation from populations of marked animals: Bird Study, v. 46 (supp.), p. 120–138.

Zakel, J.E., and Reed, D.W., 1984, Downstream migration of fish at Leaburg Dam, McKenzie River, Oregon, 1980 to 1983: Oregon Department of Fish and Wildlife Information Reports, number 84-13, 17 p.

Appendix A. Markov Chain Results from Fish Released in Cougar Reservoir, Oregon, 2011.

Table A1. Transition probabilities of hatchery and wild Chinook salmon released in Cougar Reservoir, Oregon, 2011, moving from one detection array to an adjacent detection array, given the previous array location during spring and fall.

		Probability of moving from current array to adjacent array													
	Previous array	1 to 0	1 to 2	2 to 1	2 to 3	3 to 2	3 to 4	3 to 5	4 to 3	4 to 5	5 to 3	5 to 4	5 to 7	7 to 5	7 to Pass
Spring hatchery	0	0.37	0.63												
	1			0.39	0.61										
	2	0.43	0.57			0.34	0.17	0.49							
	3			0.57	0.43				0.47	0.53	0.18	0.08	0.74		
	4					0.54	0.19	0.27			0.16	0.12	0.72		
	5					0.63	0.09	0.28	0.44	0.56				0.99	0.01
	7										0.33	0.13	0.54		
Spring wild	0	0.61	0.39												
	1			0.43	0.57										
	2	0.34	0.66			0.30	0.17	0.53							
	3			0.56	0.44				0.52	0.48	0.16	0.09	0.75		
	4					0.46	0.12	0.42			0.19	0.07	0.74		
	5					0.63	0.04	0.32	0.52	0.48				0.95	0.05
	7										0.34	0.15	0.51		
Fall hatchery	0	0.65	0.35												
	1			0.41	0.59										
	2	0.25	0.75			0.41	0.10	0.47							
	3			0.44	0.56				0.41	0.59	0.26	0.10	0.64		
	4					0.49	0.16	0.35			0.22	0.19	0.59		
	5					0.50	0.08	0.42	0.30	0.70				0.97	0.03
	7										0.26	0.13	0.61		
Fall wild	0	0.71	0.29												
	1			0.47	0.53										
	2	0.23	0.77			0.42	0.11	0.47							
	3			0.44	0.56				0.29	0.71	0.30	0.08	0.62		
	4					0.70	0.11	0.19			0.20	0.33	0.47		
	5					0.61	0.05	0.34	0.36	0.64				0.76	0.24
	7										0.32	0.17	0.51		

Table A2. Markov model comparisons for movements of hatchery and wild Chinook salmon released in Cougar Reservoir, Oregon, spring 2011.

[Models assuming a one-step Markov chain movement from one array to an adjacent array were compared to a full model that assumed a two-step Markov chain. Positive Delta AIC values indicate the model was supported (S), and negative values indicate the model was not supported (NS)]

Model	Hatchery			Wild		
	AIC	Delta AIC	Model support	AIC	Delta AIC	Model support
Full model	176.71	0.00		117.02	0.00	
M010=M210; M012=M212	192.24	-15.53	NS	131.00	-13.98	NS
M121=M321; M123=M323	320.45	-143.74	NS	118.34	-1.32	NS
M232=M432;	259.19	-82.48	NS	117.25	-0.23	NS
M232=M532;	533.67	-356.96	NS	133.73	-16.71	NS
M432=M532;	192.87	-16.16	NS	117.33	-0.31	NS
M234=M434;	175.51	1.20	S	115.46	1.56	S
M234=M534;	242.57	-65.86	NS	122.15	-5.13	NS
M434=M534;	219.80	-43.09	NS	116.59	0.44	S
M235=M435;	273.78	-97.07	NS	115.96	1.06	S
M235=M535;	360.51	-183.80	NS	122.28	-5.26	NS
M435=M535;	174.81	1.90	S	115.83	1.19	S
M343=M543; M345=M545	175.93	0.78	S	115.03	2.00	S
M757=M357;	401.50	-224.79	NS	128.88	-11.86	NS
M757=M457;	266.50	-89.79	NS	120.35	-3.32	NS
M357=M457	176.44	0.27	S	115.03	1.99	S
M753=M353;	320.20	-143.49	NS	124.50	-7.47	NS
M753=M453;	272.64	-95.93	NS	117.78	-0.76	NS
M353=M453;	175.95	0.76	S	115.11	1.91	S
M754=M354;	214.80	-38.09	NS	116.99	0.04	S
M754=M454;	175.75	0.96	S	116.41	0.62	S
M354=M454;	186.24	-9.53	NS	115.11	1.91	S

Table A3. Markov model comparisons for movements of hatchery and wild Chinook salmon released in Cougar Reservoir, Oregon, fall 2011.

[Models assuming a one-step Markov chain movement from one array to an adjacent array were compared to a full model that assumed a two-step Markov chain. Positive Delta AIC values indicate the model was supported (S), and negative values indicate the model was not supported (NS).]

	Hatchery			Wild		
Model	AIC	Delta AIC	Model support	AIC	Delta AIC	Model support
Full model	176.71	0.00		117.02	0.00	
M010=M210; M012=M212	192.24	-15.53	NS	131.00	-13.98	NS
M121=M321; M123=M323	320.45	-143.74	NS	118.34	-1.32	NS
M232=M432;	259.19	-82.48	NS	117.25	-0.23	NS
M232=M532;	533.67	-356.96	NS	133.73	-16.71	NS
M432=M532;	192.87	-16.16	NS	117.33	-0.31	NS
M234=M434;	175.51	1.20	S	115.46	1.56	S
M234=M534;	242.57	-65.86	NS	122.15	-5.13	NS
M434=M534;	219.80	-43.09	NS	116.59	0.44	S
M235=M435;	273.78	-97.07	NS	115.96	1.06	S
M235=M535;	360.51	-183.80	NS	122.28	-5.26	NS
M435=M535;	174.81	1.90	S	115.83	1.19	S
M343=M543; M345=M545	175.93	0.78	S	115.03	2.00	S
M757=M357;	401.50	-224.79	NS	128.88	-11.86	NS
M757=M457;	266.50	-89.79	NS	120.35	-3.32	NS
M357=M457	176.44	0.27	S	115.03	1.99	S
M753=M353;	320.20	-143.49	NS	124.50	-7.47	NS
M753=M453;	272.64	-95.93	NS	117.78	-0.76	NS
M353=M453;	175.95	0.76	S	115.11	1.91	S
M754=M354;	214.80	-38.09	NS	116.99	0.04	S
M754=M454;	175.75	0.96	S	116.41	0.62	S
M354=M454;	186.24	-9.53	NS	115.11	1.91	S